simply...LIFE

Back where you belong

by Kevin M Blosser

ACKNOWLEDGEMENT

Special thanks to guys like C.S. Lewis, Don Miller, Wayne Jacobsen, and other "out of the box of typical religion, thinkers", who have captivated my own imagination by their styles, insights and writings. Thank-you Connor for your help in writing this and most of all your friendship. Thanks for sharing him Claire and Chloe. Big thanks to you Laurie, my bro and my friend. I would go to war with you any day. Thanks Mom and Dad for all you've sacrificed in order to give me your best.

Most special thanks to my wife, Dana, and my two daughters, Dani and Cayley, who have been so patient and supportive, and who have inspired me the most to write this. In a day and age when love for God and each other has become acceptable as lukewarm, I hope you will never accept lukewarm as normal. I hope you will always remain free from the chains of tradition and religion, and will use your freedom to choose the adventure of living in The Father's love; I hope you'll choose Life.

... that you may love the Lord your God, listen to his voice,
and hold fast to him. For the Lord is your life.
Deut30:20

 FriesenPress

Suite 300 - 990 Fort St
Victoria, BC, V8V 3K2
Canada

www.friesenpress.com

ISBN
978-1-4602-8086-7 (Hardcover)
978-1-4602-8087-4 (Paperback)
978-1-4602-8088-1 (eBook)

1. RELIGION, CHRISTIAN LIFE, PERSONAL GROWTH

Distributed to the trade by The Ingram Book Company

TABLE OF CONTENTS

Preface 1

Introduction 4

The Instinct 9

Where it all began 13

Hungry... 24

God with us 37

Clean slate 55

Honestly Speaking 69

Christian 83

What do you really know? 107

Playing the Odd(ball)s 120

The heart of the matter 131

Less is More, (more or less) 143

All My Heart 158

Loving a Father 167

Pack Light 179

About the Author 191

PREFACE

Do you want more? Do you want to know God as Father and live in his love more consistently? Life in him will take you there. I hope this book will help to get you there as much as it has me in putting it together. No, no, no, I don't have it together, that's not what I'm saying, but this has been the best time of my life. It has forced me to spend more time with him in quiet, asking more questions, listening more frequently, and going more places. It has brought me into the lives of countless new friends over the past few years, and a lot of their friends.

I have watched first hand now on many occasions, how taking the time to befriend someone changes the course of their life. I too have benefitted from their friendship with me, changing my course, heart first. I've never really fancied myself a writer and I never planned to write a book. To be honest, I find it rather unlikely, but for the love of a Father that has, through the centuries, specialized in working with the *unlikely*, and pulling off the *impossible*. Ultimately, this book wrote itself as life happened. I hope you'll enjoy being a part of it; life, that is.

INTRODUCTION

My travels over the past number of years have introduced me to a diverse cast of characters. Some appear to be doing well, with good incomes, nice cars, comfortable homes, and membership at a nice church. Yet in the middle of relative comfort and perceived security, something is missing; the joy, peace, and contentment they've always longed for in everyday living is proving to be elusive.

Others are dangling on the fringes, drawn to what traditional Christianity seems to offer on paper; attracted by a rumor of acceptance by a close-knit family. They *show up* religiously, yet still remain conspicuously alone, stuck on the outside looking in, for now.

Then there are those who have tried but have given up on what has typically been considered traditional or mainstream. Tired of the *unnatural* and impersonal, put—on, stage event based Christian culture. Tone-deaf to the religious language of "Christianese", in the world outside of the church building, they no longer identify with the label of "Christian," and feel ominously adrift. They're totally down with knowing a connection with God but they won't be doing religious activities anymore. Many appear to be moving on.

Then there are those who are kind and compassionate lovers of God and lovers of people. They lived, breathed, and led within the walls of the institution—and they were good at it—but along the way they realized that the task of doing church became overly burdensome and impersonal; the *task* of *ministry* burning them out, stealing their joy. Now they move almost exclusively on the outside of traditional church life, living freely, loving without walls or reservations, anytime and anywhere. Misunderstood by much of the *mainstream*, they seldom defend their position, but allow their love to do the talking. They are done with the traditions, and are "affectionately" known as the, "dones".

Jesus himself was misunderstood. In his day, religious leaders constantly hassled him for where he went and what he did or did not do on the *Sabbath*; they called him a drunk and a glutton, and they questioned his choice of comrades: smelly fisherman, criminals, tax collectors, and prostitutes who would sit at his feet, at peace for the first time in forever, basking in the warmth of his unwavering acceptance and compassion.

Jesus didn't come to bring a new religion or even to modify an old one for that matter. In fact, when you look at how he spoke to the *propagators* and *enforcers* of religion and the offence they took with being called *a brood of vipers,* sons of hell, and freshly painted tombs (shiny on the outside but full of death), it sounded a lot like *religion* didn't care much for Jesus, and Jesus didn't have much use for religion.

The freedom which accurately depicts the *greatest story ever told,* scares religious leaders. Religion works great for those making the rules and running the show, but ties heavy loads on people's shoulders and religious people are not willing to lift a finger to help anyone (Matt23:4). Whereas Jesus said, "come to me personally, learn from me, give me your heavy load and take mine which is light, and you will experience rest and peace" (Matt11:28-30). Jesus was inviting people to toss the human constructs derived to gain God's approval, and instead, run to Father personally, as a loved child, at rest in his love and affection.

We who call ourselves Christians often misrepresent what *following Jesus* is, often forgetting *why* and *what* our faith is built on—and because of that, we inadvertently shut the doors to God's kingdom in the faces of the people who want and need him most. To the leaders and teachers Jesus said:

You shut the door of the kingdom of heaven in people's faces. You yourselves do not enter, nor will you let those enter who are trying to. (Matt23:13)

Or perhaps what we're *really* doing is excluding them from a structure of man-made philosophies built on the back of the greatest story ever told, while burying the beauty and simplicity of the Gospel (good news); the Father for us, Father with us, Father's Spirit and voice alive in us, for us to navigate life's complexities.

People of all ages and walks of life fall through the cracks as they look for a semblance of relevance and purpose. In my travels I see it daily, up close and personal. Deep down I think all people hope God would in some way reveal himself to them. Some through a message given through a burning bush, a sign in the clouds, or a moment of unparalleled revelation—but most would be satisfied with another human-being simply showing legit interest, friendship, and compassion, rather than critical observation, in conjunction with an impersonal "fix me" plan.

THE INSTINCT

A few years ago while living in Central America we had the opportunity to observe the releasing of a bunch of baby sea turtles that had been hatched from eggs, found on the beach, and prepared in an incubator.

Sometimes where the mothers had laid their eggs, they had become exposed on public beaches and when these eggs were found by the "turtle people" they would gather them and incubate them in a controlled environment, and release them into the wild when they were ready.

Because of the infants sensitivity to the light they had to be released after dark, on the sand about twenty feet from the surf. They were born in the dark and away from the water but it was amazing how natural instinct moved them to head for the waves as they somehow recognized the sound of the breaking surf as their path to freedom.

———◦———

"They did not receive the things promised, they only saw them and welcomed them from the distance. And they admitted that they were aliens and strangers on earth. People who say such things show that they are looking for a country of their own. If they had been thinking about the country that they left, they would have had opportunity to return. Instead, they were longing for a better country – a heavenly one." Heb11:13-16

———◦———

On the evening we got to witness their release, the surf was fairly rough and the baby turtles really got pounded, and many were washed back up onto the shore time and again but eventually and persistently they made it out past the beach break and out to the open water.

———◦———

For the flesh desires what is contrary to the Spirit, and the Spirit what is contrary to the flesh. They are in conflict with each other, so that you are not to do whatever you want." Gal5:17

———◦———

Like a newborn sea turtle, it seems we too have a desire or an instinct that is woven into the fabric of our souls that is longing to return to where we belong. As we approach the water, having been pounded time and again by the violent surf, we weigh the options; give it one more shot to push through the waves and head for the open seas to our destiny, or retreat to what appears to be the safety of the deserted beach. At first sight the beach appears to portray security and tranquillity, but lurking behind the tall grass in the cool and blackness of the night, the jungle is teeming with predators, looking for fresh meat for their next meal.

Parting Shot

This is the inner conflict that affects us all. While God's Spirit is trying to direct us into our life's true purpose and destiny that only he knows, our senses and what we would call logic, is moving us towards personal comfort, cheap and temporal pleasures, and the illusion of safety and security; none of which satisfies, and ultimately leads further from our absolute greatest potential. The senses and God's Spirit are in constant conflict. When it comes to giving directions, they are not friends even though the senses do there darnedest to convince us that any and all forms of sensual self-indulgence is beneficial for mind, body, and spirit.

WHERE IT ALL BEGAN...

The first part of this chapter could be viewed by some as being somewhat elementary. I would be doing a bit of an injustice to others, however, by making the assumption that the first part of the equation is common knowledge on the way to the conclusion. If you find yourself thinking "I've heard the story a hundred times, get on with it already!", I would encourage you to skim this chapter, grab what may have value to you, and disregard the obvious. The purpose here is to establish common ground to ensure we are all on the same page and footing as we proceed. I would be getting ahead of myself if I prescribed a solution prior to clearly identifying *the root*, and where and how the breakdown came about in the first place.

In short, we have found ourselves living a life alienated from the most essential personal relationship. This was not the original design; however you interpret the creation account in Scripture, one thing is clear to all of us, there was a point in History where this world was good. Life was good. Relationships were good. Physical, spiritual and emotional health was good. Then after exercising the God given gift of free will, a decision was made to exercise independence, consumed by a desire to be like God, and life has never been the same.

I don't know if you've noticed, but as a result, we are not living in a world that can often be described as "good" any longer. Life is hard. Relationships on every level are broken. Our bodies are prone to chronic pain and disease. Our spiritual lives seem critically lacking, and emotionally, we are fragile. According to CNN, anti-depressants are the most commonly prescribed drug in the United States as mental health illness and disorders are skyrocketing. I don't think I need to go into great detail to try and convince you that much of what we experience in this life is far from good. And yet there is hope, a *light* that shines through the bleakness of our brokenness illuminating the way back to where we once belonged.

As the story goes...

In short, and as the story goes, a long time ago there lived a very satisfied couple, the first couple of humanity, known as Adam and Eve. Their home was located in the most perfect environment imaginable, as it was situated in a garden-like setting, amongst all sorts of fruit trees, lush gardens, rivers and streams for great fishing, and an abundance of wildlife to enjoy right outside the front door.

Throughout any given day, they could be found walking and talking and living with their Father and creator in perfect relational balance and harmony. Since all they knew was peace, contentment, and goodness, they had no idea and no thought as to why life was, it just was what it was, and so with no contrast or comparison, they just rolled along in complete and total ignorant bliss.

Having been created and always remaining in their Father's presence, living in this perfect garden, and likely never even experiencing a bad day or even a headache for that matter, they didn't know what they didn't know; all their needs were met, life was good, and it didn't matter why.

How long the arrangement of living in perfect bliss lasted is anyone's guess. This utopia could have lasted 40 billon years or 40 minutes, the Genesis account does not divulge, but one day, and in the blink of an eye everything would be forever changed. Maybe it was boredom, maybe it was curiosity, maybe it was both or something altogether different, but simply living in the love and provision of the Father was no longer enough and they went for option "B", personal knowledge and independence.

The couple known as Adam and Eve would have had no idea of the Pandora's Box they were opening. Along with the *opening of their eyes;* they (became obsessed with the idea) were blinded to what they had by the thought of what could be; *being like God,* of knowing both good and evil, whatever that meant. Once they pulled the trigger, it says in Genesis, the first thing they felt before anything else and even before they spoke again with God, was shame. As soon as they had stepped out of the Father's provision for them their *eyes were opened*, and they realized they were *exposed*. Naked and embarrassed, they went and found a good place to hide (Gen3:7-8).

Every thought and possibility that they had never even considered as good before, when good was all there was, was now complicated by competing *voices*, twisted thoughts and new awareness of a destructive alternative for anything and everything. Without exaggeration, they must have thought they were losing their minds.

One day Adam was calm and secure in his understanding that God was there as a friend and provider, and the next he was running away from him like a madman, hiding in the underbrush in a pile of leaves, ashamed of looking and feeling naked. He went from knowing that he had it all to the realization that he had just discovered the opposite feelings of *peace* and *contentment* in a matter of moments. Suddenly he discovered brand new confusing feelings of shame, worthlessness, and fear and he must have wondered how he would ever be able to make it a day on his own.

It...

Human-kind, by design and in our original living arrangement, had a sense of personal worth genuinely intact. We naturally had *it* because we relied solely on the Father for everything, and the Father was dependable to provide everything that was necessary. *It* wasn't even something that we knew or was recognizable because *it* was naturally there simply by association, until the relationship between God and people was *disrupted* by the choice for independence. No longer relying on Father God, but now personally knowing the difference and making decisions just like God did. Unprepared and ill-equipped, bobbing in an ocean of uncharted possibilities of good and evil, it immediately became clear that things would be different, very different.

That decision, in a way, put God out of work as the One who knew the difference and who would stand between us and the really tough decisions and human complexities. God had provided and protected the most vital personal need, our sense of self-worth, but not anymore. By our choosing, Father took a step back and painfully granted his children the ability and independence, allowing us to manage and sort out our value, provision, and purpose. This also initiated things like, worry, self-doubt and insecurities of self-worth because now it was all on us. It was up to us to make things happen, and to make the decisions necessary to provide for ourselves everything that Father had always provided through a natural and trusting relationship.

For Adam and for men going forward, his independence would also become his torture and his prison. He would now know the burden of being the one expected to provide for his family. Being out in the garden was no longer a joy and a pleasure, but would be toilsome; work, work, work, just in order to bring home enough, just to get up the next day and do it all over again with no help and no relief in sight. When there were questions or problems it was up to him to have the answer and the solution whether he had it or not.

Eve, instead of feeling this perfect love of God meeting her every need alongside her life-mate, now turned to her newly broken down and ashamed, basket case of a man, to provide her with personal worth, and identity, which he was never equipped with to provide for himself or anyone else in the first place.

We've been stuck in this rut of attempting and failing to meet this need of personal worth by our own means ever since. Looking to be valued and validated by the approval and actions of other tarnished, broken, and disenchanted humans, rather than resting in and relying on a Father, whose love and intentions for us have always been healthy, constructive and perfectly honorable.

"They are darkened in their understanding and separated from the life of God…" (Eph4:18)

Could it be that our *self-interest nature* and the human desire to pursue, at any cost, an impossible rumor of *happiness* by way of the natural person's sensual survival routine, is driving us deeper into a self-centeredness that leaves us routinely feeling like we're chasing our tails by pursuing more *stuff*, generally unhappy, busy yet bored, and dissatisfied with most everything and everyone around us?

Our unchecked sensual twists and bends will eventually and always show themselves in the way we relate with others. Maintaining marriage promises, "in sickness and in health", and keeping life-long commitments for improving life together, is beginning to sound more and more like an unbelievable fairy-tale. We want instant, and we want easy. We want justification to walk away, and we want deniability here in the *land of opportunity;* opportunity to get whatever we want whenever we want it, twenty four-seven. This is easy-breezy unchecked sensuality, and this is what is happening to the North American culture and family. The *good news* is that it doesn't have to be.

———◦———

Come to me, all you who are weary and burdened, and I will give you rest. Take my yoke upon you and learn from me, for I am humble and gentle in heart, and you will find rest for your souls. (Matt11:28—29)

———◦———

Jesus clearly models a life of great potential and quality living, by initiating love, acceptance, and compassion, and instructs us to also live in, and out of that same love, acceptance, and compassion of the Father; the way it was originally designed for all of us.

———◦———

Love one another. As—I have loved you—love each other. (John13:34—35)

———◦———

"What we really need is somebody who loves us so much we don't worry about death, about our hair thinning, about other drivers pulling in front of us on the road, about whether people are poor or rich, good looking or ugly, about whether we feel lonely or about whether or not we're wearing clothes. We need this; we need this so we can love other people purely and not for selfish gain, we need this so we can see other people as equals, we need this so our relationships can be sincere, we need this so we can stop kicking ourselves around, we need this so we can lose all self-awareness and find ourselves for the first time, not by realizing some dream, but by being told who we are by the only being who has the authority to know, by that I mean the Creator." *Donald Miller(SFGKW)*

———◦———

"I have learned the secret of being content in any and every situation, whether well fed or hungry, whether living in

*plenty or in want. I can do it all, anything, through Him
who gives me strength." Phil4:12-13*

Mixed signals...

Father God is in the process of renewing things; renovating
so to speak. He wants us to know how valuable we are to
him. He wants to start there. I admit that in the middle of the
storms of life, the turmoil, the pain, and the tragedy, there
could appear to be mixed signals being sent.

Maybe you're thinking—"How can you speak of God's
love in the middle of all life's tragedy and turmoil? I would
think that a loving God would protect me from evil. How
could a loving God allow genocide and starvation and all
the terrible things that happen to relatively *good* people?
Wouldn't a God of love save the *good people* from the evil in
the world?" A God of love would absolutely love to save all
people, but the choice for being rescued, by coming back to
him is up to the individual.

God gave us choice; life with him, by design, or of death
outside of that design. No different than a tree with roots
planted in, and nourished by moisture and nutrients found in
top-soil. Pull the roots out of the ground and eventually the
tree dies. A human was designed to remain planted in God,
but God did not force himself on us, and gave us the option

to choose. God wouldn't be the only game in town if choice were to mean anything, for love to mean anything. There has to be an obvious alternative. God's love itself would lack definition without contrast; no thankfulness, no compassion, not even the knowledge of joy.

A Father giving his children the choice between life in him, or having the knowledge of both good and evil in order that they would truly be *offspring* and not *pets* or *robot's*, is incredible love. Maintaining robots and keeping pets would have been a whole lot easier than watching your kids hurt and kill each other I imagine. There are always going to be good and bad choices, but I accept the possibility of bad choices if that means I also have the opportunity to see and live in the good this world has to offer, the best way that I can.

Parting Shot

This life is a twisted cocktail of the consequence of both the *curse* as well as the *blessing* of knowledge of good and evil. It was our obsession for knowledge that got us into this *beautiful mess*, and if we'll pay some attention, it is God's Spirit that is hoping to provide us with the way through it and ultimately beyond it. It's a tough race but for those who will push the boundaries of excellence to the finish line; we win. We get it all; absolute goodness and the knowledge to know the difference.

I think Jesus taught us that we have a Father who loves us more than we know & if we could sort that out we would know how to treat each other. (Wayne Jacobsen quote)

HUNGRY...

The people's champ...

I remember a number of years ago now, coming home late from another exhausting day filled with wining and dining and schmoozing. As usual my wife and kids met me at the door with a hug and a kiss, but I was barely able to even look at them. I remember feeling so pre-occupied, and "distant" and "empty" about basically everything in my life including her and the kids. I said a quick "hi", gave them a token hug and kiss, and skulked into my "lair", closed the door behind me, and sunk into my favorite chair.

I remember putting my head in my hands, closing my eyes, taking a deep breath, and trying to take inventory of my life. "What is wrong with me?? I shouldn't be feeling bad, I had it all. I had a great job, lived in a big house, always drove a new vehicle, had a great wife and two beautiful daughters, was involved at the church fulfilling my "religious obligations" and had the personal "religious angle" to life covered, or so I thought.

I was the guy, leading, teaching, singing....with passion. I was pretty much the peoples champ when it came to passionately doing what I thought was worship and encouraging others to do the same, but somehow instead of realizing a growing peace and contentment, and being transformed into a more loving husband, father, friend, and business owner, all I was feeling was exhausted by it all.

-----------⊙-----------

I have come that you would have life, and have it to the full. (John10:10)

-----------⊙-----------

How could a person appear to be so completely devoted to the cause of Christianity on Sundays, emotionally embracing the total program, including the promise of possessing peace that goes beyond comprehension, and yet still be feeling so empty? I was doing everything that anyone had ever shown or told me to do in order to be a superstar Christian, but if this is how being a superstar Christian felt, I didn't want to be a superstar anymore. My entire life felt like an endeavor of mundane futility. There had to be more than *this*, but for the life of me I couldn't figure out what I was missing. All I felt was ripped off; I had either missed the point altogether, or someone was lying.

———◦———

Do not work for food that spoils but for food that endures to eternal life. (John 6:27)

———◦———

The word...

I recently sat down with a good pastor friend of mine and asked him what he considered to be spiritual food and how a person is spiritually fed. He thought for a brief moment, then pointed to what Jesus said to Satan when he was alone fasting and being tempted out in the desert:

Man shall not live on bread alone but by every word that comes from the mouth of God. (Matthew 4:4)

I couldn't argue that. If Jesus said it then I believe it to be true, but without making assumptions, what does that really mean?

We really do begin to live good again when we live by the words that come from the mouth of God. But what about those words? Is it just about hearing the words regularly, or committing the words to memory that make the words of God alive, breathing, and food to live by? Jesus doesn't explain further on this occasion but a bit later on he does. He actually has a lot more to say about it.

Food you know nothing about...

One day, while Jesus was walking back to his hometown, he stopped at a well for a rest and a drink of water. While he was there resting, a Samaritan woman from a nearby town also stopped at the well to get some water. Noticing her water bucket, Jesus asked her if she wouldn't mind drawing some water for him as well since he had no bucket with him.

The nature of their conversation soon expanded spiritually, and Jesus introduced her to a new freedom of living and a way to know and worship God in Spirit and in Truth. He explained that it was a personal affair, and not dependant on attending *holy* buildings, bowing on *holy* mountains, and keeping traditions. It was a radical new twist from what she had believed; that *common people* could have direct interaction with God at any time, and in life's most natural settings. She was reassured for possibly the first time in her life that Father God was for her as she was, as she is, any-time, any-where. He approved of her and loved her, period; he wanted the best for her, he was not against her.

After returning from buying some food in a nearby town, Jesus' posse of followers arrived back on the scene. Whether the woman was still there and the disciples interrupted the conversation, or if the conversation had just ended and the woman was just leaving and was heading back to town, his followers unfolded their picnic blanket, called Jesus over, and began to eat.

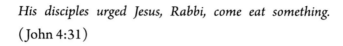

His disciples urged Jesus, Rabbi, come eat something. (John 4:31)

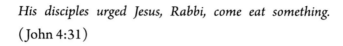

My guess is that since she was *just* a Samaritan, they probably thought they were being good *wingmen* by interrupting the conversation so Jesus would have a good reason to walk away from this *dog* (this was the current cultural view of Samaritans) of a woman and have some lunch with *the boys*.

But Jesus, possibly even a bit perturbed at the interruption, had other things on his mind other than a baloney and dill pickle on rye sandwich, and he said to them, *"I have food you know nothing about"*. This of course confused his bro's and they discussed between themselves how he might have found some *food* while they were gone. That afternoon, Jesus revealed value to a new friend while taking the time to explain to her how she could freely approach God, and to his old friends he modeled how to be fed in a spiritual sense, among other things.

This teaching moment was about spiritual food, but it wasn't just about spiritual food, it was about life. This was about a life lived out of the love and personal presence of the

Father and living in the center of the Father's plan, which was even more satisfying than eating a meal, or being entertained by a football game, surfing the net, or going shopping. Living personally, in and through the Father's love was more satisfying and trumped anything, even food.

Jesus also seized an opportunity in a very natural setting to *break down walls* in order to convey the love of the Father and begin a friendship with a most unlikely person, someone who in a cultural sense would be considered an adversary.

As we go along we'll talk more about breaking down walls and building friendships as a lifestyle but for now I want to focus in on what Jesus had to say about the enjoyment of the *food his companions knew nothing about.*

Free lunch...

I'm unclear as to how things got to where they are today, however, what Jesus went on to say about *being fed* looks and sounds nothing like our current standard routine. This, I believe, could also explain why a good many of us feel like there should be something more to the Christian experience; often feeling like we're literally being starved of something but are unable to place our finger on it.

So what is spiritual food according to your current understanding? How do you believe a person is fed spiritually? How do you personally attempt to be spiritually fed? What have you been told? I would make a calculated guess and say that the most commonly accepted means of being *fed spiritually* would be the following:

- Go to a local church that preaches the word of God, and listen to solid bible preaching and teaching.

- Get into a small group bible study.

- Don't just rely on someone doing it for you—do your part by reading your bible for yourself at home.

- Pray, memorize scripture, journal, and sing songs that recognize and Honor God.

Many of us are familiar with verses that teach us how important it is to be nourished by the Word of God (1 Peter 2:2, Hebrews 5:12–14, and 2 Timothy 3:16 are just a few examples). But is it possible we've neglected the totality of the message that clearly states that there is much more to spiritual nourishment than hearing, reading, and studying what we have typically called the word, and the truth?

The aforementioned activities, as good as they are, in the proper context and purpose are a great place to start, but will not directly satisfy our God-given appetite and will not in and of themselves bring about true spiritual growth and health—not according to what Jesus says next.

Jesus said, *my food is to do the will of him who sent me and to finish his work.* (John 4:34)

Notice that what Jesus called spiritual food was not a free lunch, nor was it something that Jesus received (such as the Father's words given to him). No, his food came from being *one* with his father, being united with him personally, hearing his voice, and honoring him by what he did with others, in and through that relationship.

If you obey my words you will remain in my love, just as I have obeyed my father and remain in his love. I have told you this so that my joy may be in you, and that your joy would be complete. (John15:10-11)

We go to hear a teaching, or sit down to read something, or sing songs and pray, and we expect to be spiritually fed simply by these activities alone. This belief, in fact, never came from Jesus at all—it was our own idea spun from Jesus' statement that man shall not live on bread alone but by every word that comes from the mouth of God. This statement alone, if not taken any further than the act of personal consumption, will leave us hungry and dissatisfied.

———◦———

"A new command I give you: Love each other. As I have loved you, so you must love one another. (John13:34)

———◦———

The rest of the story...

If spiritual food according to Jesus is when we are participating together with the will of the Father and to finish that work, what is doing the will and work of the Father? What exactly was Jesus doing at the time when he filled these guys in?

Jesus was outside the religious meeting place and he was hanging out with someone who his culture considered to be a whore and a cross-bred Samaritan dog. His actions proved that she meant more to him than what was dictated by the cultural norm. He was personally engaged, explaining and showing her the simple way to the Father, proving her worth by giving her his undivided time and attention.

Jesus wasn't simply giving her words of truth—he was introducing her to the person that is the Truth, and is the Way, and is the Word, and is the Life, by breaking down walls so she could know him personally. Not a religion, a theory, or a philosophy for her to remember, but a Father that loves her and wants her to know and walk in his love in a personal way. That bolstering of her self-worth would change her life.

Emanuel (God with us) would sure have had the right and religious clout to challenge her behaviour and beat her up a bit or guilt her in regards to her multiple divorces and adultery, but instead, Jesus lets her know that he is aware of all the trash in her life, and she is loved by he and the Father regardless. *"We can still be friends. Not just when, and if you get your act together, but in this moment, at any moment".*

———◦———

Dear children, let us not love with words or tongue but with actions and in truth. This then is how we know that we belong to the Truth, and how we set our hearts at rest in His presence. (1 John 3:18–19)

———◦———

I don't believe this was just another quiet, eat lunch and take a nap sort of afternoon, as Jesus was attempting to get this across to the friends who were with him. This relationship was the heart of the message that would restore life, and this conversation may have gone on for hours. I think Jesus was totally jacked—he was energized, he had just been filled with a *food* that outweighs any other; he put his arm around someone and he gave them hope. Judging by his reaction, I believe the personal interaction and the potential it had to transform her life and the lives of the people in the town where she lived had Jesus so fired up—the last thing he was thinking about was a sit-down lunch with the fellas.

Guys, open your eyes! Don't just sit around listening for the Father's words, planning what we might do someday! Look around us right now—did you see that woman? She's so broken. There are people in need of the knowledge and understanding of the Father's love all around us! The harvest fields are ripe right now! This is the food that satisfies, this is my food—you can keep your sandwich. (Paraphrased, John 4:32–38)

Parting Shot...

—————◦—————

I tell you the truth, anyone who has faith in me will do what I have been doing. He will do even greater things than these. (John 14:12)

—————◦—————

From a practical perspective, take a look at your own life and experiences: Is it not more satisfying to give to someone or to help someone in need, or to fight for someone else, rather than do nothing or to do for your-self alone? When we are loving others in the same way, it is also spiritual food for us, aligning us in complete cooperation with the plan and personality of the Father and of others who are also invested in the restoration of life; not out of duty, obligatory service, or basic obedience, but from friendship, son-ship, daughter-ship, and being loved. That alignment, spiritual intimacy, fellowship with family, and fellowship with the Father is known personally. It is powerful, and it leads to peace, contentment, and confidence in all aspects of life, regardless of circumstances. It is the food that Jesus speaks of. It develops life.

GOD WITH US

I will ask the Father, and he will give you another
Counsellor to be with you forever—the Spirit of Truth . . .
if anyone loves me, they will obey my teaching. My Father
will love them, and we will come to them and make our
home with them. (John 14:16 and 23)

Since the beginning it has always been God's desire to be
present with His people. We see this to be true in the creation account up through to the present. In Genesis ch.3 it
says that God "walked" in the garden. Adam and Eve were no
strangers to the presence of God. Even after this relationship
was fractured by sin, God still desired to be with the people
he created. His presence was made manifest to Israel by the
cloud that led them by day and the fire at night. It was witnessed by the Ark of the Covenant and the Temple, where

God's presence resided. In the New Testament Jesus Christ (Emmanuel-God with us), entered into our world and lived among us. Now God the Holy Spirit lives inside His people, bringing the presence of God to our very hearts. Although the relationship will not be fully restored this side of Heaven, with the Holy Spirit in our hearts there is now a sense in which we can (like Adam and Eve once did) walk in the presence of God.

———◦———

Having believed, you were marked in Him with a seal, the promised Holy Spirit, who is a deposit guaranteeing our inheritance until the redemption of those who are God's possession. (Epheshians1:13-14)

———◦———

In today's culture that is being overwhelmed with social media distraction, we're faced with an ever increasing problem. Even when we're alone physically, we're not alone in thought anymore and I do not believe that is inadvertent or by coincidence. I think most people today are afraid to face the silence of their soul, fearful of what they might find, so a lifestyle of personal meditation and interaction with the Father is avoided altogether. That is a shame because moving through life with a clear mind and few distractions is when the Father's voice is heard and known with the greatest consistency.

———◦———

Whether you turn to the right or to the left you will hear a voice saying, "This is the way, walk in it." (Isaiah 30:21)

———◦———

Hearing directly and experiencing the influence of the alive, active, simultaneous movement of God by his Spirit is what moves us into our greatest life purpose and potential. It is in these moments when he takes ordinary words and places them in the correct sentences at the correct moment. It is he who opens mouths and silences them; it is he who opens the ears of the deaf; it is he who directs feet down his paths; it is he who causes feet to be still. He gives and makes words and action beautiful, melodic, and harmonic when they are introduced and initiated at His discretion and in His timing. He is the ultimate maestro of life's orchestra; without his direction, life often feels like a mundane exercise in futility, littered by cliché, and the remnants of dreams of what could have been.

This timing and alignment of God is a vital part of the great mystery and adventure that is missing today in the lives of people calling themselves *believers*. We have many false perceptions of who God is, how God works among us, *being spiritually fed*, and that is just naming a few. We have become complacent in a religious culture that wants to hear words and say words, but is losing its stomach to *walk* in them, and when we miss the application aspect of the equation, we've missed it all.

Rather than walking slowly and steadily with God's Spirit and walking as he walks, we have adopted a logical business-like or governmental approach. We now hire men and women to do the *jobs* that are part of *the code* for every single individual to take ownership of and be involved with in a personal way. If we're a part, we're a part; if we're a spectator, we're a spectator, and this life is not a spectator sport at any level. The original church in its purest form is not to be attended or watched; it is the hard hitting game of life, lived loved.

This is the entire point of God's Spirit living in us today, working through us; he and us united in life and purpose; walking together, it's a raw and beautiful thing.

When he, the Spirit of truth, comes, he will guide you into all the truth. (John 16:13)

God's Spirit in our life keeps us from missing the forest for the trees, and keeps the horse in front of the cart. He takes us from the limitations of simply reading and hearing words to understanding the heart of the message of the words, and takes us from having knowledge of the letter of the law to understanding the intent and true meaning or spirit behind the law.

It is the living out of the written words, by the ever-present direction and empowering of the Living Word, which takes us full circle and brings about true understanding, knowledge, and application, unifying us with the Father and his plan, and as we've already discovered, is also the energizing spiritual food that Jesus speaks of.

Being a part of and doing (walking) what is said and written is what makes those words alive, active, and sharper than even a double-edged sword (Hebrews 4:12). It is what makes words and theories, relevant and proven in any generation, culture, or language. Without the doing, we're really just a bunch of highly educated theorists who possess nothing of interest to a generation that needs to be part of something they can touch, something of substance, something tangible.

It is the daily, practical, and natural lifestyle of walking in this truth that makes God's message and plan all this and more.

I will give you a new heart and put a new Spirit in you. I will remove from you your heart of stone and give you a heart of flesh. And I will put my Spirit in you . . . (Ezekiel 36:26–27)

It's the Father's unflinching love and compassion that balances the combination of authority, fatherhood, and friendship, that he, by his Spirit, would love to teach us—especially when it comes to parenting and other forms of real-life leadership. It is the same love that vehemently protects and defends the cause of the widow, orphan, the helpless, the needy, and the lonely, but is secure enough that it does not feel compelled to lift a finger to defend itself or gain personal recognition.

This is the love that God's Spirit would like to grow in us as we truly, willingly, and intentionally expose our lives to him. Thus we will be transformed by his love, bit by bit, keeping in step with him by following the instructive voice of his Spirit as we move along.

In the Western world, it certainly does appear as though the direction and life purpose of many of us calling ourselves Christian may have become somewhat clouded.

If this were a business, and it is not, but if it were it would be the people business that we're in. While our capitalist culture is generally geared to focus more on quantity (maximum return for minimal investment), God's Spirit is all about the quality of the process required for the healing and renewing of his children.

To take it a step further, if this were a business it would actually be the friendship business. The quality *friendship thing* these days, is undoubtedly, a relational problem affecting a great majority of our culture and society. We seem to have lost complete touch of the quality ingredients that go into healthy and true friendship, both person to person and person to Spirit, but the Father has not lost touch.

———◎———

We have not received the Spirit of the world but the Spirit who is from God, that we may understand what God has freely given us . . . we have the mind of Christ. (1 Corinthians 2:12 and 16)

———◎———

No fear...

A number of years ago I was a part of a study group, looking to better understand the natural, day-to-day interaction of God's Spirit in the lives of some of the earliest friends and followers of Jesus, based on the accounts written by Luke in the book of Acts. We were a very diverse group, with backgrounds in both the conservative as well as the more liberal spiritual points of view. We all still came to the conclusion: that the most common visible interaction of God's Spirit exhibited practically in the life of the revolution's earliest participants was boldness. Boldness to walk away from what was comfortable and easy and predictable, while getting into real-life situations that were way over their heads. Boldness to go anywhere and do anything at any time at the moment of God's direction, according to his plan and purpose.

They had *tasted something* and truly wanted to see and be a part of God's plan. Trust, leading to boldness, was a primary *gift* that would help them get over their fears and complacency, propelling them into what had previously seemed unthinkable. That's not to say there were no bizarre and incredible instances of the miraculous, because there certainly were, but boldness was at the forefront.

There are also many other spiritual gifts that are intended for us to use in the development of God's kingdom. Paul said that the Father gives gifts of wisdom and of knowledge, of faith, and of healing. He will provide supernatural strength and power for miracles, and give someone just the right word at just the right time. He will give the ability to some to speak languages that the speaker does not even know or understand, and to others will give interpretation and the ears to hear. But we shouldn't limit Father God with this simple list. He can and will give any gift imaginable or unimaginable to anyone at any time, but don't expect to receive any spiritual gift from the Father without the boldness to step out and trust him to do what he says.

Peter experienced the miracle of standing on water because he had the boldness to step out of the boat when Jesus told him to hop out, take a chance, and live a little. The apostles received insight and miracle upon miracle because they had the boldness to remain in the heart of the anti-Jesus storm in Jerusalem as Jesus instructed them.

Even during the centuries of the old covenant, Moses, after initially running away from Egypt, was given boldness so that he might return to face Pharaoh in order to lead his brothers and sisters out of slavery. While God did perform many miraculous signs and wonders in order to influence Pharaoh, it was the gift of boldness that got him started.

Abraham was called the father of faith because of his boldness to live by and trust in God's promise to him. Daniel and his three friends exhibited boldness by standing their ground, not caving in to popular culture, and were found safe in the middle of a fiery inferno and in a lion's den. Elijah experienced the miracle of consuming fire from heaven when he had the boldness to stand up to the false prophets, build an altar, and douse it repeatedly with water, while leaving his matches at home.

David, a boy standing in front of a giant while warriors hid, exemplified boldness. Rahab a prostitute, hiding spies, risked her very life and was thereafter known as a heroine of faith. Elisha, Ezekiel, Gideon, and others . . . on and on the list goes citing simple, ordinary, and weird people that God had a special plan for due to their willingness to get involved, He started them off with boldness.

In all their situations it was God who did the ultimate heavy lifting, but he uses ordinary people to share in his plan. He gives us boldness as we keep in step with him by his Spirit in order to do what must be done.

I praise you Father, Lord of Heaven and earth, because you have hidden these things from the wise and learned, and revealed them to little children. Yes, Father, for this was your good pleasure. (Matthew 11:25–26)

Radar...

A while back I got a call from a friend at around seven o'clock on a Sunday evening. He wanted me to get in my truck and drive forty miles to pick up a couple of large items he had purchased earlier at a farm auction. I'm not sure how well this friend knows me, but if he knew me well enough he would know that my Sunday evenings are sacred and off-limits when it comes to chores and physical exertion other than lifting my fork. It is my time to wind it all down before the rigors of a new week. So you can imagine that I was initially perturbed by his request to get off my butt to be his personal delivery guy. I think what really perturbed me was that I was in the middle of writing a book about living in and through a Father's love and the missing link of personal sacrifice, which is required for building extraordinary friendships. Now I had to put my money where my pen was and I was initially not so happy about it. *Who shows up at a farm auction intending to buy things with no means to getting things home other than a*

Toyota Corolla? I wondered. Well, my friend just did, and now his problem had become mine.

So while I worked out this perturbing request, making arguments in my little mind, I was interrupted by a rather subtle prompt *that this may be bigger than an oddball request* for a Sunday evening home delivery service due to the lack of someone else's transportation management skills. So I not so happily agreed, fell out of my hammock, and headed for my truck. As I hopped in, I noticed a few text messages on my phone sent by another friend who I had been attempting to connect with for a few weeks. Again, there was a small prompt, a notion that I should see what he was up to, right that moment. *Maybe,* I thought, *he'd like to go on a small road trip into the country.*

Turns out I was right—he was looking for any reason to get out of his apartment, and in less than fifteen minutes we got on the road and headed out. We chatted as we drove to the farm where we would pick up the water tanks, and enjoyed each other's company as we loaded them up while our other friend looked on, providing carrying instructions and helpful loading tips. Back on the road again, we headed back to town to unload. After all that work we decided that a pizza would go down nicely, so we headed over to a pizza joint and continued working out the mysteries of God and life together. It was exactly what my friend needed that day, and it was exactly what I needed, too. I didn't even spend ten minutes talking to the friend who made the strange request that got me out the door and on the move in the first place, but it was the catalyst required to get me where I needed to be in spite of my personal philosophy of, "no one messes with my Sunday evenings!" It also went a long way in the developing of a friendship that continues to work towards bringing out the best in each other.

This isn't taking down a giant and is far from spending a night in a lion's living room, but this is also how the Father works in everyday life as we attempt to keep in step with him by his Spirit. Someone makes a strange request in order to get someone else out the door in order to connect with someone else who had previously been totally off the radar. We just need to keep in step by always remaining ready and available to recalibrate our location, which will bring us to others who had previously been off our radar screen.

———— ·⊙· ————

The Spirit helps us in our weakness. We do not know even what to pray for, but the Spirit himself intercedes for us with groans that words cannot express. And he who searches our hearts knows the mind of the Spirit, because the Spirit intercedes for the saints in accordance with God's will. (Romans 8:26–27)

———— ·⊙· ————

The point...

If and when we are walking by God's Spirit, over time, we will want to love our neighbour, whoever that may be, in the same way that Jesus described when he told the parable of a Good Samaritan.

The only directive given to us by God was to come to him and know his love and to love each other, and to not become twisted or polluted by the popular culture (James 1:27). This was the Spirit behind the law and the Ten Commandments. Since we did our best through the centuries to negotiate a human-logic-fueled, bogus give-and-take version, Jesus came and set the record straight, inspiring people to write it down. Then he made his Spirit available to walk with each of us so we would never be without his words and presence and to give us confidence of his affection for us, so we'd have the courage to burn the ships and never look back.

The reason the Son of God appeared was to destroy the devil's work. (1 John 3:8)

The Holy Spirit will teach you all things and will remind you of everything I have said to you. (John 14:25)

As I have loved you, so you must love one another. (John13:34)

Now that you know these things, you will be blessed if you do them. (John 13:17)

Read those verses again, slowly. Do you see the connection here? Why did Jesus come? What did he say? What did he do? What did he tell us to do? What is the role of the Spirit? And when are we blessed? What is blessed?

So many stories are written in that book of the bible about actions and consequences—stories about having the free will to choose; to build a house that either weathers storms or collapses, of a guy finding something of such incredible value he would give up everything he had in order to own it, of unfaithful noblemen being thrown out of feasts and beggars taking their seats, of honouring the king by caring for lepers, and of eternal reward for temporal sacrifice. They are all woven together into the perfect picture by perfect understanding by God's Spirit through daily, consistent, and intentional acknowledgement and interaction.

If we've done any reading or studying of what God communicated through the Old Testament prophets and the life of Jesus, this message of God's love for us (and by us living in this love we would love others the same), is consistently woven throughout. It is crystal clear, and is actively reinforced in one's life by the indwelling Holy Spirit if knowing his heart and keeping in step with the Father is what we truly want.

We need to personally get to know the Father's love for us. A great place to start is by reading about Jesus as he is the exact representation of God (John 14:7 and 9-10). Take your time and read Matthew, Mark, Luke and John—the books that tell all about the life, words, plan, and way of the Father, exampled through the life and personal interactions of Jesus.

Read slow and ask the Father to reveal his heart and purpose as you go, in order to gain personal understanding.

Then check out the complementary writings of the later books of 1John, Peter, and James, and the letters Paul wrote, especially the letters called 2Corinthians and Galatians. If you want to see just how personal the Father gets with people by his Spirit; the hunger and dedication of a man who initially hated Jesus before he got to know him, read the inspiring book of Philippians.

Love, by Jesus' definition, driven along by God's Spirit, is not passive and does not retreat. It is fearless and does not calculate risk versus reward; is relentless in the pursuit of his objectives, and his objectives are you and me, the sketchy neighbours along the road.

Parting Shot...

—————◈—————

I know the plans I have for you, declares the Lord, plans to prosper you and not to harm you, plans to give you hope and a future. Then you will call on me and come to me, and I will listen to you. You will look for me and you will find me when you look for me with all your heart. I will be found by you, declares the Lord. (Jeremiah 29:11–13)

—————◈—————

If we truly want to know the Father and have him share in our lives, he is happy to come to us and live with us, by his Spirit. But he comes as a complete and total gentleman. He doesn't go snooping around, making a bunch of demands, and telling us about all the stupid, ugly stuff we have in our home; and he doesn't dump on us for all the stupid things we do and say. He comes in with a kind smile, at complete ease, regardless of the condition of our home. He takes a genuine interest in us as he listens to all of our stories, plans, dreams, failures, and hurts, regardless of the type of language we may use. He doesn't come with a hidden agenda, he's not in any hurry to speak, and he's not in a hurry to go anywhere else.

The more time we spend with him, the more we see in him of what we ourselves hope to be. We begin to talk less about ourselves and ask to know more about him as we truly desire to become more like him in every way. As we continue to ask, he is happy to answer, and over time, shows us, tells us, and gives us all that we'll need to keep moving along. A whole new kingdom that we never knew was even possible opens up to us. By his way, the blind receive their sight and the deaf their ability to hear; the lame walk, and the beaten, bruised, and broken, are healed. The outcasts are welcomed, the lonely find friendship, and the widow and the orphan are given a family and a home.

———◇———

Does it make you a king to have more and more cedar? Did not your father have food and drink? He did what was right and just, and so all went well with him. He defended the cause of the poor and needy, and so all went well. Is that not what it means to know me? declares the Lord. (Jeremiah 22:15)

———◇———

CLEAN SLATE

Bitterness is like drinking poison and hoping
the other person dies from it.

———◆———

Let us fix our eyes on Jesus, the author and perfecter of
our faith, who for the joy set before him endured the cross,
scorning its shame... Hebrews12:2

———◆———

Do I really believe that my un-checked, self-centered failures
had me staring at, and ultimately floundering in the hopeless-
ness of death apart from God? Do I believe that figuratively,
I was standing at the gallows with the noose around my neck
when, out of the crowd, a stranger walked up and said to the
hangman, "Let him go, I'll take his place"? Do I believe this
stranger then looked at me, and seeing the terror on my face,
with a grin and a wink said, "Hey, no worries friend, I got this,
I'll see you in a few days". Do I believe that a few days after

I watched them kill him, he came to me and told me about his Father's plan to rescue all the other kids—and that I too could have this *life* if I would get to know him, follow in his footsteps, and learn to love the people of this world?

If it is possible, as far as it depends on you, live at peace with everyone. (Romans 12:18)

What's done is done...

One Sunday, while I was sitting in a traditional church, the lights dimmed and a video on the big screen began showing random news feeds and video clips. One of the first was of Richard Nixon claiming that he was not a liar, another was of Bill Clinton saying, "I did not have sex with that girl". There was a clip of Ted Haggard speaking against homosexuals, followed by a clip of a foot protruding from a public bathroom stall. Another clip was of Toronto Mayor, Rob Ford, denying the use of crack cocaine, along with news feeds and headlines of many other disgraced public figures.

As I watched I looked around and noticed people laughing as the video went from clip to clip, from scandal to scandal. And then something came over me and I almost felt sick to my stomach as I realized that we, a group of people who are to be known by mercy, compassion and forgiveness, were watching the worst moments of someone's life, on a big screen, and were somehow being amused by their humiliating failures.

In that moment a picture came to my mind of what it would be like to be sitting in a room with a bunch of people, friends—family—strangers, and we dim the lights and a video comes on, and we all get quiet, and on that big screen was an oversized streaming video of me committing one or more of the worst moments of my life, in HD for everyone to see. I could only imagine the incredible embarrassment and shame I would feel if I had to relive my worst moments in front of you all. Don't get me wrong though, I'm not ashamed of my worst moments where they currently sit; life happened, I've done what I've done along the way, but that was yesterday.

Fully understanding the love of the Father for his kids, his grace, acceptance, and approval regardless of what we were or even of what we believe we still may be, is more than enough of a reason to let those who have wronged us, off the hook. If we believe all this, a default position of forgiveness is a no-brainer. End of chapter, case closed.

I tell you: love your enemy and pray for those who persecute you, that you may be children of your Father in heaven. (Matthew 5:44)

The sandbox...

I think one thing that we need to always remember is that I am not, and you are not, the only kid in the *sandbox* that the Father cares for. We need to get our heads around the idea that this kingdom of God works as a family, and God is Father to us all. When one of my children is off the wall about something and it affects the other one negatively, as their dad, I don't want my offended child to retaliate against their sibling. I want them to show each other grace and respect for the unity of the entire family by working things out and moving on.

I want them both, healthy, happy, and prosperous in this lifetime, no matter what. I want to develop in them an emotional strength and confidence to "play their own game" as I modelled for them and taught them, regardless of the games being played around them, for this is to their benefit.

I want them to realize they are living in a culture of grace, that their own imperfections and offences are regularly being overlooked, in order to see and to know by experience the transforming power of grace. This is what the Father and Jesus exemplified and participated in fully for the rest of God's family to see and know.

The Father loves us all. His desire is for all of us to be reconciled, and there are matters that he has asked us to not take into our own hands. He knows a lot about taking a beating because of someone else's incorrect actions in order to send a message of love and value—a message that will transform a heart. That's the strategy at this time. It's what love and forgiveness does: it humbles and transforms the hearts of everyone involved.

Fair play...

Having a heart willing to forgive will also come down to personal perspective, and specifically our understanding and expectation of two words: *deserve* and *fair*. Ultimately we want what we think we deserve, and based on our point of view, we want someone else to get what we think they deserve based on a given situation—basically what we believe is fair.

So, let's talk about fair. Is life fair? If we ever hope to find consistency and justice in this lifetime we must all be playing on the same field, playing by the same rules, with the same equipment, with the same opportunities, and perfect officiating. Receiving the outcome based on this equality played out would be fair and then all could get what we deserve.

Fair is everyone eating well, living in a nice home, living in a peaceful neighborhood, and safety for our children. Fair, is everyone driving a nice reliable car, having a loving spouse, working at a good job, cash in the bank, good mental health, and disease-free physical health, among other things. If this is the case for everyone on the planet, then we could say that life is fair, and we would not require things like understanding, grace, and compassion. White picket fences for everyone.

How do I get what I deserve? I must perform an action, pay an amount, or provide a service to receive something which is considered equal and fair by all factions involved. That's fair across the board.

Does a kid get what they deserve by being born into a nice stable family living in a peaceful country, going on to play professional baseball and marrying a supermodel? Does another kid get what they deserve when they are born in Cambodia and sold into sexual slavery at eight years of age because their family is dirt poor? Is that fair? Did everyone here get what they deserved in life?

The *rules* are no different just across the street from us or in the house next door. One kid's dad celebrates New Years with him by playing and shooting fireworks, while just around the corner one kid goes out to the barn to discover that his father has shot himself. One kid's father calls him *buddy* and adores him, while another kid's father calls him *a-hole* and beats him regularly. I apologize for being blunt, but this is the reality, people. This is happening in our neighborhoods, my neighborhood to be precise, and those are the names that people are literally given while they're children in our towns and cities.

So what do we really deserve? What is the rule of "deserving" even based on, if not on perfect equality? What is really fair? How do we bridge the gap when none of us has received what we deserve, whether good or bad? We bridge it in the same way that the Father has built a bridge back to us: with unconditional love... and mercy... and compassion... and forgiveness.

Jesus spelled it out earlier when he said that not one of us is in position to remove crud from someone else's eye because we have so much in our own that we can't even see straight (Luke6:42). Imperfect, broken, and tarnished people are in no position to keep score when it comes to *wrong doing*, nor can we legitimately appoint ourselves as the authority on whether or not people should be let off the hook for doing wrong.

Why do you look at the speck of sawdust in your brother's eye and pay no attention to the plank in your own eye? (Matt7:3)

For freedom...

We humans are very complex when it comes to feelings, emotional balance, and the things we think we need to do or to hang onto in order to preserve and/or establish our value and identity.

Forgiveness serves more than just some religious and obligatory purpose of being obedient to God just for the sake of looking like good kids. Since we're on the topic, let's talk about what the deal is with obedience for a moment or two.

We always need to remember what the point of obedience is from the Father's perfect perspective. We too often have a misguided and misinformed view of God's laws, his ways, and his reasons; which limits our potential and freedom.

God has given us *laws* for one reason alone: he loves his kids, all of them. God's laws aren't imposed to control us or keep us from fun and enjoying freedom. They are for the exact opposite reason—they are for freedom, and are intended to protect us from ourselves and each other. There wasn't one command given from God to Moses that would take away from my or my neighbor's quality of life. They all improve it. And now a new and better way has been introduced by Jesus that has over-written that old law.

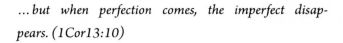

...but when perfection comes, the imperfect disappears. (1Cor13:10)

The air was crisp, and out in the country this night it was peaceful and quiet; no fighting or quarreling, no buzz from traffic, no sirens, and no dogs barking. As I walked through the trees and looked up into the starlit sky, I thought to myself, "can it get any better than this? Such an incredibly beautiful creation, my Father who loves me, my wife who adores me, my girls were safe, my friendships solid", and I wondered how heaven could get any better than this moment.

Do you know what heaven is? I clearly don't think I do, but if heaven were simply living on this planet minus the self-centredness that causes greed and violence and theft and abuse, etc., this earth and life would seem pretty perfect to me. It's not rocket science to see the problem here, and Father God has made himself available to us as the perfect solution.

Above all, love each other deeply, because love covers over a multitude of offences. (Peter 4:8)

By design...

Forgiveness is about experiencing a fresh start and a new day, a sunrise. What happened yesterday happened; there is no going back, there is no erasing, there is just a new sunrise tomorrow. A sunrise is best enjoyed when we have nothing more on our minds than the beauty of a sunrise. Forgiveness is like a blank canvas to an artist to begin fresh, with new hope, with new vision and a new freedom.

In this "people business" there will most definitely be bumps and bruises, dents, and scrapes along the way. Forgiveness is the letting go of the things of this world that stand in the way of personal relationship between us and God, and us and people. If we want to enjoy life in the midst of the struggle, it is a must. Remember, the words that Jesus spoke were not meant for a select few righteous folks. None of this love and forgiveness business is just a Christian concept. Jesus himself is not just a Christian concept either, if that makes any sense. This is and has nothing to do with a religion or doing things religiously and it probably should not have ever been given a name. Jesus was hated and killed because he stomped all over religiously motivated behaviour done in his Father's name, during his time on earth.

This is the real, living designer of the *machine* giving instruction as to its limitations, capabilities, and potential if operated according to design. This is the Father of the human race showing us the way to peace of mind and great living, not schooling in the *shoulds* and *shouldn'ts* of God-pleasing, religious activity.

The bible is not some religious rule book meant to be read by religious people who hang out in religious buildings with religious symbols. This is not a message for the "good enough." The beauty of it, is that none of us are good enough, yet the Father still *believes in us,* and wants us restored to *wholeness* regardless.

This is the Father's message of hope, transformation, reconciliation, and restoration of all mankind, meant for good living for all.

We are all equals, and we're all in the same boat. If we choose to be individuals who protect and serve rather than take pleasure in pointing out others' faults and demanding their punishment, it will go a long way toward building God's Kingdom here on earth—of family and of friendship.

Parting Shot...

Forgiveness restores the dignity of both perpetrator and victim; it zeroes out the account, so to speak. I'm not owed, you don't owe me; we move on, start again, and maybe get it right next time. Otherwise, we attempt to move forward in a state of emotional and spiritual deficit from the guilt and/or resentment hanging over us, regardless of whether we are perpetrator or victim. That makes moving forward extremely tedious if not eventually impossible.

It's important to note that forgiveness and freedom are very much linked together. The love of God incorporates a compassion/grace/forgiveness-first protocol. While we were enemies, Father God was not pleased to hurt or punish us but initiated love, knowing some would still reject him (Romans 5:10). Jesus, while he was being killed, said this about his killers:

"Forgive them Father, because they don't know what they're doing." (Luke 23:34).

If those killing Jesus should be forgiven because they didn't know what they were doing, even though it would appear to be obvious that they did, then most of us on any given day, also do not know what we're doing, and are prime candidates for grace and forgiveness according to Jesus' example.

People are broken; we are all broken for one reason or another, and motivated by things that we don't even know or understand about ourselves, and especially each other. Regardless, God loves all his kids in spite of our failures, so we Honor and please him, and bring spiritual and emotional freedom to ourselves and others, as we take the highest road, as we forgive.

We often set our expectations too high and give ourselves and others way too much credit to do *the right thing* and in doing so, set each other up for imminent failure and disappointment. Freedom is found as we invest in, and experience healthy and honest friendship that accepts people regardless of offensive and, or personal failures.

Draw close to the Father, get to know everything about him, personally and intimately. By simply drawing near and remaining in his love, his style will become our default position from which we choose mercy, compassion, and forgiveness.

HONESTLY SPEAKING

Dirty clothes dropped on the floor don't pick themselves up, get washed, folded and put back in the correct place when we leave the room and close the door. The mind also is a series of closets and filing cabinets for the events of life, so to speak, that properly or improperly store every sight we've ever seen, every word we've ever heard, every thought we've ever had, and every feeling we've ever known. Proper organization and waste management is vital.

<hr />

"So if the Son sets you free, you will be free indeed." John 8:36

<hr />

Even Steven…

The "freedom" that Jesus wants to give us, is not at first so much the ability to refrain from wrong doing or protection from feeling wronged or hurt, although through the process and following his example that aspect will also improve. The initial freedom is about emotional and spiritual health in learning better about our Father, ourselves, and others, and a new way or covenant between us, and realizing the outlet to properly dispose of our "trash".

During his life on earth, one of the first things that Jesus appears to do is put people on an even playing field; he re-introduces equality among all people. To those who were weak, he made them feel strong. To those who believed themselves to be powerful, he humbled them.

---

*"Blessed are you who are poor, for yours is the kingdom of God. Blessed are you who hunger now for you will be satisfied. Blessed are you who weep now, for you will laugh...
But woe to you who are rich, for you have already received your comfort."*

Woe to you who are well fed now, for you will go hungry. Woe to you who laugh now, for you will mourn and weep." Luke6:20-26

Outcasts were accepted, and the diseased were made healthy. He then put wrong doing into proper perspective for the first time, since the idea of an eye for an eye was accepted as proper.

"If any one of you is without sin, let him be the first to throw a stone at her." John8:7

Jesus puts everyone on an equal playing field physically and emotionally. Then he puts us all on the same playing field spiritually by essentially saying, the issues in your own life make you totally unfit to see the faults in others clearly and unbiased. No one is in position to fairly judge the heart of another person.

And then he speaks to His purpose for living on this planet:

"... I didn't come to judge the world, or to count people's sins against them; I came to save them regardless..." (John12:47 & 2Cor5:19 paraphrased)

Basically, "I'm not here to judge you, but I'm here to make a way for you to have life again. The time for justice will come based on what you did with what you were told and given, but not today. Today I show you a better way."

Love and let live...

For the first time since the law had been given to Moses many hundreds of years earlier, a break was given for the consequences of wrong doing. The law appeared especially hard on people when they did wrong, so people lived scared to death (literally), and overly legalistic and paranoid about any little thing they did that might not be seen as perfect in the eyes of God, and which in that day was enforced by a self-justifying, self-righteous, self-serving religious institution.

All this "self" business was alive and active because at the time they knew of no other way to deal with their individual wrong-doing and guilty consciences other than...you guessed it, themselves. Once a year they killed a goat or a dove or two to make amends for the previous year, but after half an hour and an argument with the wife, they were back on the hook for another year.

They took ten commands from God to Moses and turned it into 613 detailed sub-commands and rules that the people diligently attempted to keep straight. Why? They had missed the point of the spirit behind the rules. They totally missed the message. The Father had seen and heard enough, so he had Jesus break it down from six hundred and thirteen man-made laws and variations of the man-made laws down to just... ..., wait for it... ...one. One point of emphasis would encompass—everything. Take care of each other from the greatest to the least, regardless of whether you are the greatest or the least, and that covers it.

———◦———

"... The Father who sent Me commanded me what to say and how to say it. I know that His command leads to eternal life." John12:49-50

"This is my command; love each other. As I have loved you, so you must love each other." John13:34

———◦———

And how would we do this, taking care of each other?
"As... I have loved you".

He elevated the small and weary, he stood up to the bully, he touched the sick, and rather than point out individual faults and failures to be corrected, he had grace, and mercy and forgiveness for the wretched. Each and every one of us, and he made us his friends in spite of our imperfections and weaknesses. This is what changes a person, regardless of whether one is on the giving or the receiving end. It's win—win—win. One may be physically fed, while the one providing food is spiritually fed, and the Father is overjoyed to see it!

Jesus looked past our wrong doing; told us to look past each other's wrong-doing, and then went to bat for us in dealing with the consequence (death) of our wrong-doing. He then also gave us fulltime access to his Spirit as an advocate to be able to communicate with him directly for friendship, wisdom, and counsel at any time. As a result, our heart goes from thinking about wrong-doing and instead moves on to greater things: love and grace, mercy and compassion, and living and laughing in the freedom of being a bit of a shmuck in the heart of Shmuck-vil. This is freedom.

"I am the gate; whoever enters through me will be saved. They will come in and go out, and find pasture. The thief comes only to steal and kill and destroy; I have come that they may have life, and have it to the full." John10:9-10

Jesus is talking about a whole different way of achieving this life that works out best as free-people, than what anyone expected, and he really surprised people with the freedom he came to revive. The Jewish people in Jesus' day and, before, had assumed that the prophesied Messiah, or deliverer, or The Christ, would save the Jewish people from the Egyptians, Babylonians, or Assyrians; in Jesus' day it was the military occupation by Rome.

Instead, Messiah came to deliver people from the burden of trying to look and feel like they were in right standing before God by their own goodness, by their own merit, by trying to keep God's perfect law which was impossible. He came to free souls, he came to bring peace (of) for the mind. He came so we could relax, in who and what we are. It would be ok; no, even better, we would actually be encouraged to simply be ourselves.

By grace, an undeserved gift of radical acceptance, regardless of lifestyle and past behaviour, Jesus set out the way before us of how we too needed to see and accept ourselves as well as the other "travelers" on this journey. Jesus coming to live on this planet was all about the restoration of our relationship with God, and a trickle-down effect that would allow one restored to love and accept our fellow man freely and without self-serving conditions, confirming their value.

As Father shows us who we truly are to him, how he sees me, and how he sees "them" we gain personal confidence of his approval and validation of our personal worth and slowly mature to where we become a bit more oblivious to the superficialities and surface defects in others.

People are a picture of diverse ebb and flow. Like a river flowing through diverse landscape and terrain, over hundreds of miles, we are rough and smooth, wide and narrow, fast moving and slow, winding and straight, and needless to say, but I'll say it anyway, very much uncontrollable and unpredictable. As we learn to accept this of ourselves and of others, we will learn to enjoy all aspects of this "river" of life regardless of our natural and, or learned preference.

One language…

A great example of "popular humoring" which is a first cousin to *little white lies*, came up one day when my buddy Darren and his wife Rebecca were over and the topic and a book they had read on "love languages" came up. I have to admit that I'm not one for *formulas* or *catch phrases*, so right from the get go, the whole idea of a "love language" in my opinion was something that would be found only in a "chick book", and that's where it probably should stay. Lo and behold and to my surprise it was a dude who wrote it, if you can believe that. I pray for that guy, his wife must monitor him closely. I can hardly believe she let him write her book.

"Love language! Are you kidding me? The whole notion would suggest that we are supposed to humor people by telling them what they want to hear in the way that they need to hear it. It promotes humoring, vague dishonesty, and enables self-centeredness by the recipient". I not-so diplomatically interjected.

"How so", she asked. "The whole idea that I or anyone else needs someone to speak to me in a way that I appreciate or like will lead people to not be totally truthful in their approach with me in other areas of life. With some people catering to my *sensitivity* (insecurity), I'll expect everyone to, and that will actually stunt my growth relationally. To make me "happy", they would humor me. I don't want to be humored. Why can't people simply accept people and their style for what it is? Don't mess around trying to act out my language, just be yourself. If I love you, I'll adapt to accept your style. Jesus' model of love should be able to handle individual and personal complexities and diversity, should it not?"

Rebecca brought up the point that people are where they are and what would it hurt, and wouldn't I be loving them by getting out of my comfort zone in order to reach them in theirs? "After all, Paul did say that to the Jews he was a Jew and to the Romans he was Roman, suggesting that he would be as versatile as necessary in order to reach people where they were at."

What would it hurt for me to do some things that I wasn't comfortable with in order to make someone else feel comfortable where they were at? Honestly, it would hurt me none. I've done it before and I could do it again. It would also teach me about the idea of putting others needs ahead of my own, which is also commendable. To make myself uncomfortable in order to make them comfortable seemed like something that Jesus would be all for. But then again maybe the win—win—win solution arises when we are comfortable enough with our-self that we don't require others to stray from being them-self in order to make us *happy* enough to receive their natural idea of a love offering.

This unconditional acceptance happens as we develop personal confidence and maturity. Life in the Father works away consistently at both maturity and confidence and when we can grow up enough to accept each-others hard-wiring freely and appreciatively, and with our insecurities fading away, this pleases our Father as well. Win—win—win.

"If you hold to my teaching you are really my disciples. Then you will know the truth and the truth will set you free." John8:31-32

Low expectations...

Would you be satisfied knowing that people feel they need to tip-toe around you? Humoring you by telling you what you like to hear, the way you like to hear it? Never really feeling safe to be transparent, and truly honest with you? Knowing that the *clam-up*, or *cold shoulder* treatment is imminent, and will be applied for as long as you feel like they've been adequately punished, when they appear to oppose your opinion, style, or *language*? I don't think any of us want to be that person. I think we would all like to be free of the relational handcuffs caused by our own insecurities and emotional fragility. We can apply pop-culture *band-aids* or we can be healed from the roots up.

While I agree that we do need to look to the interests of others and be considerate and speak lovingly, which is sometimes stronger and at other times gentle, and never use this freedom we have as an excuse to do and say what we please to others because they should receive us unconditionally;

learning to speak cute and delicately and or expecting the same from others, is not the point I hope to get across here.

The bottom line is this: books about love languages and finding mutual points of consideration, make some very good starting points for those at the earliest stages of relationship building and or reparation, but Jesus' way of love trumps all and if we start and settle for less, we'll never grow up to be what we could be in him.

I'm not saying that we shouldn't be considerate when communicating with others. We should, but concentrating on speaking peoples love language, and wanting mine to be spoken, is operating from the wrong end of the spectrum based on Jesus' teaching. It can also set a bad precedent in all of our other relationships outside of marriage. If we don't get this in the proper order we will always be operating from a position of feeling scorned, or offended in one way or another, and we will never enjoy the adventure of diversity or the friendship that Jesus speaks of from relationships, that make life great.

I tell you, do not resist an evil person. If someone strikes you on the right cheek, turn to him the other also. If someone wants to sue you and take your tunic, let him have your coat as well. If someone forces you to go one mile, go with him two miles. Give to the one who asks you, and do not turn away from the one who wants to borrow from you.

You have heard it said, love your neighbor and hate your enemy, but I tell you; love your enemies and pray for those who persecute you, that you may be sons of your Father in Heaven." Matt5:39-44

When we understand clearly where it is that we truly stand from our Father's perspective, realizing his completely sufficient approval and acceptance on the days when we can't even accept our-self, this changes our perspective drastically. This becomes inner-confidence, and it transfers directly into freedom from the anxiety caused by our own attempts to acquire security from well-intentioned, yet extremely unreliable, people. Once we begin to live in and exercise this freedom, it doesn't take long to realize that it will never matter again to us what *'language'* is being spoken to us by others, or if nothing is said at all.

I'm not a psychologist, and I certainly will not be confused with a genius, but I have come to this conclusion based on studying the words of Jesus and observing people: our human condition and the disease that is killing this life of potential abundance, has a great deal to do with our expectations towards other people and the things we think we need from them rather than recognizing and living in the love and freedom to be ourselves, found by knowing and living in the love of our Father

This changes the order of the equation from "depending" on the quality of the offering given, to possessing the ability to unconditionally accept an individual by placing the same value on that individual as the Father has on me, rather than dissecting the behaviour and, or style of the individual, and therefore approving or rejecting as it suits me. Knowing and living in the Father's love allows us to take off our suits and throw out our masks, while welcoming and encouraging the same from others.

To believe that how people treat us is at all relevant to how we are to receive them or respond to them is absolutely false according to what Jesus says. It is a blatantly false notion that has been too widely accepted in Christian circles, and has been robbing people of God given power, confidence, and freedom in relationships, stunting them as obligatory Christian "relationships" rather than growing them into something much stronger, into friendship. Love is not a conditional response; it is unconditional and is repetitive initiative.

Parting Shot...

Our standing with God has nothing to do with anyone other than us, and he shows that he loves us enough to die for us, even though and when we don't love in return. Once we personally know and experience the extent of the love that the Father has for each one of us, regardless of our performance, we will then truly begin to understand the freedom which allows us to be completely genuine with our blemished skin, and allow others that same freedom.

CHRISTIAN

If you hold to my teaching you are really my disciples. Then you will know the truth and the truth will set you free. (John 8:32)

What does the word *Christian* mean in today's Western culture? If you were to ask ten people, you could easily get ten variations of definition. Does it mean that a person is a follower of some superior moral code of ethics that, if observed, correctly places someone one step ahead of the others in a moral competition? Is it being polite, courteous, a political association? Is it giving a homeless guy a couple bucks, buying a coffee for someone ahead of you in line at Starbucks, being just a generally nice guy or gal? Does it mean that we believe in going to church at Christmas and Easter and on the occasional Sunday—or maybe every Sunday without fail—tithing, dressing up in our finest, paying homage to God, singing spiritual songs, or listening to some encouraging words that make us feel better about ourselves and our circumstances? Is it loving our neighbor as we would ourself? Is it all of the above? None of the above?

Whatever you have done to the least of these brothers and sisters of mine, you did for me. (Matthew 25:40)

Running to win...

There is an eighty-year-old lady living in Cambodia where thousands of children, ranging in age from eight years old to adult, are being sold by their families to the local mafia to work in the sex trade. Marie, was widowed in her fifties, and retired by the mission organization at the vibrant age of sixty-six. Alone, she started over, took her life savings and used her pension to establish a centre to care for people with AIDS. Since there were no anti-viral drugs at that time, she watched every person she cared for die, which left her with new opportunities, and facing a whole new set of challenges.

Her patients, who had become friends, passed away and left behind children who were now orphans. Marie cared for them, providing them with education, value, and a life purpose as well as bringing in and providing a home and hope for other children rescued from the sex-slave industry. She currently houses over 500 children. She hopes that number will one day reach 1000. Again, remember—today she's over eighty and going strong!

I could not have even imagined that a lady at eighty could have as much spunk as Marie Ens if I had not met her myself. Marie is living as an immortal. This is it. This is Christianity alive and well in the most terrible times.

Foundation...

———⬥———

I tell you the truth, the son can do nothing by himself. He does only what he sees the Father doing. (John 5:19)

———⬥———

In the first century, one of the earliest records of the word *Christian* was recorded in a town in Greece called Antioch. It was here that disciples, friends, and followers of Jesus grew into a community and were first called *Christian*. Initially it appears that the term *Christian* was meant to be a derogatory nickname or label, but it was soon adopted as an unofficial handle. I don't think they were really looking for a name for what was going on. After all, what do you call living in the love of your Father and loving others in the same way you are loved? I just call it *life*.

I imagine it was a title they wore humbly and without shame. With every new bit of sneering and the slanderous way that "the haters" said "Christian," they must have been reminded of their "first love," and of the seriousness of the mission that Jesus had set before them and modelled: for his "friends" to continue what he had begun—as his representation on earth, as he himself had represented the character and wishes of his Father.

<hr>

God was reconciling the world to Himself through Jesus, not counting peoples wrongs against them. He has also committed to us the ministry of reconciliation... as though God were making His appeal through us. (2Cor5:19-20 my paraphrase)

<hr>

Jesus didn't use or instruct others to identify as *Christian,* or any other title for that matter. Since he was initially identified as a teacher or Rabbi, he connected what he was about with the people who were down with what he was teaching and modelling in his day, by initially using words like *disciple* and *follower.* He often challenged those who identified themselves as followers, to consider what *being* a follower meant at the core. He instructed them, and he modeled the application, and when their lifestyles didn't add up to what they were calling him or themselves, he called them out.

Why do you call me Lord, Lord, and not do what I say? (Luke6:46)

As the days of walking with them, and teaching them face to face, was reaching its climax, he introduced a new twist to their relationship. He redefined the relationship, and he called them something that no one possessing religious clout in that day would have ever even dreamt to call those under their authority. He called them friends (John15:15).

As I...

I know that typically, there is certainly more than one way to get things done, but when it comes to following Jesus there is one denominator which remains consistent; *do as I do.* It's what a follower does. Let's look further at what the life and foundation of *Christian* consists of according to Jesus:

Now that I, your Lord and teacher, have washed your feet, you also should wash one another's feet. I have set you

an example that you should do as I have done for you.
(John 13:14–15)

———◦———

I know what you're thinking, "the foundation of Jesus' message is . . . washing people's feet? Are you serious?" Yes and no.

What Jesus was trying to get across was not that we should hold fast to literal feet-washing traditions and ceremonies. If it were, that in itself would be an extreme enough exercise for most of us—especially if you've ever seen some of the feet I've seen, including my own after a day of working in the dirt wearing flip-flops.

No, it's more than that, much more. Jesus was teaching about a way of life, about a kingdom way of life, of leading by example; of coming beneath someone and humbling yourself to show another human their value. He showed that giving love, and acceptance, was not contingent on a person's performance or social status. Jesus was the big man on campus, so to speak, yet he got down low, and washed dirty, stinky feet; the job that was typically the job of a slave or servant. Even though Jesus knew that Judas would betray him, he still washed his feet; though he knew Peter would deny knowing him on three occasions soon to come, he washed Peter's dirty feet, too.

Being a friend of Jesus has more to do with having the confidence to choose to love first and ask questions later, rather than attempting to protect personal interests or perform rituals and fulfill obligations.

I understand the initial confusion that people faced as they were buried under the laws of Judaism, custom and traditions, the ritual temple worship of God, and being highly dependent on the priests as personal intercessors. However, all that changed with Jesus, and changed even further when the Father sent his Spirit to live and interact with individuals in a most personal way.

We have been and are being equipped moment to moment by his Spirit to (function) love in natural settings, among the best of the best, and the worst of the worst. There's no need to try and act the religious-looking part, or come off as "having it together."

If we aren't careful, *Christian cliché land* can get us so focused on trying to *act* like Jesus that we neglect to simply draw near to him personally, becoming the best *me* that I can be, according to his design, direction, and purpose for the person he made me to be. We only need to be what we are and who we are: works in progress, loved by God, and people who love each other with compassion and unparalleled generosity as a result.

As I have loved you, so you must love one another. By this all men will know that you are my disciples if you love one another. (John 13:34–35)

Reckless abandon...

People who are immersed in God's *agape* (the Greek word that speaks of the highest form of love and charity between God and humans, and humans for one another) will gravitate towards doing extraordinary things atypical to the majority, going beyond what is typically considered safe or comfortable. People who are not immersed in this sort of "careless" and "reckless" love normally make decisions based on common sense, natural human logic, and attempt to calculate any and all potential risks.

A Christian can afford to make lifestyle choices that the majority may consider as reckless and careless? Yes—remember, God is immortal; he can't be killed—and so is the love that characterizes his nature. Under his banner, we as *followers* are also immortal; which translates into the potential of incredible freedom from any earthly fears. This is not just a possibility; it is the reality for anyone who wants to follow Jesus, living in the love of the Father.

God will give to each person according to what he or she has done. To those who by persistence in doing good seek glory, Honor, and immortality, he will give eternal life. (Romans 2:7)

Of all the people on this planet who would do the most dangerous and self-sacrificing jobs, none are as secure and well-equipped as a friend of Jesus. The immortal can afford to live every day with reckless abandon in the Father's love. These lives of reckless abandon will serve as signposts for those who are lost and are in desperate need of finding their way back home.

By both listening to and observing Jesus, we are able to get to know him. When we really get to know him, we both admire and have affection for him—enough that it moves us to follow his example personally, strengthened and encouraged by the Spirit of God as we go. Knowing and experiencing personally his compassion and grace consistently, naturally moves us to approach neighbours, family, co-workers, strangers, even—especially the *crustier* people, with the same love and compassion.

If one is simply told the words of Jesus, but doesn't see the speaker exemplify compassion, grace, and mercy, they will have difficulty absorbing a challenging message that appears to fly in the face of good logic, doesn't make all that much sense and doesn't really sound like all that much fun. Speaking love, can mean many things to many people; being love is exactly what it is, and opens the door of the heart, for the love of the Father to enter, reside, and move about.

It's worth noting that while Jesus showed himself to be powerful, kind, confident, and fearless, he never used those traits to protect or promote himself; instead he propped up those who needed it most.

———————

If I glorify myself, my glory means nothing. My Father, whom you claim as your God, is the one who glorifies me. Though you do not know him, I know him. If I said I did not, I would be a liar like you, but I do know him and obey his word. (John 8:54–55)

———————

The source of Jesus' strength and confidence and fear-lessness stems from this: *I do know him, and I obey his word.* Everything starts here; it is the foundation of the knowledge and confidence of immortality, which leads to:

... anyone loving me, will obey my teaching. My Father will love him, and we will come to him and make our home with him. He who does not love me will not obey my teaching. (John 14:23)

Can you see a pattern here? This is very important to take note of. Jesus isn't saying these words to elicit or oblige obedience from his followers. He's not saying this with guilt or a manipulative tone. We often hear people say things like, "If you love me you'll do this," or "You guys need to do that," or "You really should do this," but this is not Jesus' tone. It is simply, cause and effect. If we get to know God and his affection and love for us we will love God; and as we love God we will be a part of what he's about. Walking with the Father may begin as childlike obedience, but maturing love goes well beyond simple acts of obedient behaviour as true bonds of friendship, daughter-ship, and son-ship are developed.

Now remain in my love. If you obey my commands, you will remain in my love, just as I have obeyed my Father's commands and remain in his love. (John 15:9)

One of the major reasons that so many of us are living such dissatisfying lives is that we have never totally understood and or entered into this complete lifestyle of *agape,* or God Love, personally.

The *McDonalds,* instant "Christian conversion experience" of praying a technical "Sinner's prayer" receiving Jesus symbolically and possibly even just romantically—confessing verbally, Jesus as Lord—often misses the point and practical-ity of a practical creator who doesn't just do stuff to do stuff and say stuff because it sounds cute and, or romantic. He said, "come to me", as a personal invitation, so that we would *come* to him. He said to *remain in my love* so we would remain in his love, and when we do, it changes absolutely everything. This is relationship language that he's using.

My command is this: Love each other as I have loved you. Greater love has no one than this: that he lay down his life for his friends. You are my friends if you do what I command. (John 15:12–14)

I think we've overlooked and neglected the possibility of an hour-by-hour friendship in the basic, natural, non-religious activity living—a lifestyle that is ever cognizant of the actual presence of God.

I don't doubt that we have some feelings of affection, and our words and songs would indicate that we do, but genuine love for Jesus is demonstrated in this way: *If you love me, I will be in you and you will be in me, and you will say what I say to you, and will share in what I'm doing in the lives of people, per-sonally and in natural settings.*

—⊷◦⊶—

"When you ask you do not receive because you ask with wrong motives, that you may spend what you get on your pleasures." (James 4:3)

—⊷◦⊶—

This idea of God being *in us* and *us in God* will radically shift how we pray. Jesus taught his friends to pray, "Father, your kingdom come, your will be done on earth as it is in Heaven." But we pray for things like safety and a successful day, and if we're honest with ourselves, we're more than likely thinking, "I'm all for God's will to be done and his kingdom come here on earth—as long as priority #1: I retain control and understanding, life stays comfortable and relatively easy, the kids stay healthy and happy, I remain employed, the car and a/c keep running, and the stock market doesn't crash." We're terrified of losing control and being in a position of not understanding the why's and the what's. We're terrified because we simply do not trust, and if we do not trust we have nothing. How well does a relationship work when there is no trust?

We have prayed for daily bread, and sure enough our Father has provided enough "daily bread" to feed the population of the entire world twice over, daily. But we are the hands that he has intended to use to distribute that "daily bread." Instead of feeding the world twice over, we instead have become fat and wasteful, taking it all for granted, feeding only ourselves, leaving those without to starve.

Our choices, both good and bad, along with the choices of others, can determine the outcome of our prayers and the prayers of those left to starve and be tortured and murdered along with their children on the "other side" of the world . . . and on the other side of our cities . . . and on the other side of our street.

. . . any of you who does not give up everything he has cannot be my disciple. (Luke 14: 33)

A friend in deed...

More than likely every one of us has been in a situation in our lives when we wound up in a time of need, and in that dark hour someone showed up and helped get us through it. We've probably also experienced moments when we could use a little help and couldn't seem to find anyone who cared enough to offer even an hour of their time.

"It was just before Christmas, and all through my house . . ." actually, it was just before Christmas and outside my house there was so much darn snow that the mice were building igloos—not great rhyming I know but you get my point.

As I was outside shovelling and pushing snow around and getting more annoyed by each new snowflake wrecking my life, it was what I could hear going on in the house that added to my annoyance big time.

While I was out there in the snow and cold, busting my butt, all I could hear and imagine coming from inside the house was Christmas music and my wife and kids in the warm house around the fireplace, laughing and ringing those Christmas bells, eating Christmas cookies, and drinking hot chocolate.

Meanwhile, this is what I was thinking: "What an ungrateful bunch of kids I've got. Where are you when there's any sort of work to be done? You just love the gifts under that tree and all the good stuff I provide for you, but you don't ever even think about what I might find helpful. All you think about is what you're getting from me, while all I do is bust my butt for all of you. Nice, thank you!"

No sooner did I entertain those thoughts than a new series of thoughts began to emerge: Is that how I treat my Father that I say I love? Am I just all about the good things that he gives, and grumbling, complaining, and disappearing when things get inconvenient or uncomfortable? What sort of son am I? What sort of friend?

———◦———

You expected much, but see, it turned out to be little. What you brought home, I blew away. Why? declares the Lord

Almighty. Because of my house which remains a ruin, while each of you is busy with your own house. (Haggai 1:9)

———◦———

As much as we *try* and *want to* put God first and love others with equality, the bottom line is that if we would get honest we would see that most often we are still the love of our lives. We are stuck in the middle ground. We've heard the truth, have tasted the truth, have been convinced through experience that Jesus' way is the best way to live, yet still hold back on loving our neighbour or even our families, as we are or would hope to be loved.

We may have patience, but only to a pre-set degree. We are kind, but only to a point that we determine. We are generous, as long as it fits our budgetary comfort. That's why we are never really satisfied with anything. We are only intellectualizing the life and relationship that Jesus presents, tainting it with a great deal of self-centeredness, rather than believing, as Abraham actively did, in God's plan—and subsequently living *in* and *out of*, according to that trust or faith.

———◦———

Seek first the kingdom of God (Matthew 6:33)

———◦———

I think if we were to look at this with our eyes wide open we would see that there are major disconnect between what Jesus said and did and what we actively do. We need to ask ourselves, "does my life even remotely resemble what Jesus spoke of and actively did as a lifestyle, truly loving and investing personally through friendship in the lives of people around me?

How many new faces outside of our typical cliques, have seen the inside of our homes, at our invitation, in the past few years? How many of them who have are we still regularly invested in today?

The apostle James said that when a person possessed "true love", *true religion* would accompany it, and helping the lonely and the least of the least and the widows and the orphans would be commonplace. Personally, not programmed, not professionally, not organized as some form of *outreach* or *ministry*, but naturally and as a typical person lives in the Father's love.

———— ⟨◦⟩ ————

You cannot fast as you do today and expect your voice to be heard on high. Is this the kind of fast that I have chosen, only a day for a man to humble himself? Is it only for bowing one's head like a reed and for lying on sackcloth and ashes? Is that what you call a fast, a day acceptable to the Lord?

Is not this the kind of fasting that I have chosen: to loose the chains of injustice and untie the cords of the yoke, to set the oppressed free and break every yoke? Is it not to share your food with the hungry and to provide the poor wanderer with shelter—when you see the naked, to clothe them, and not to turn away from your own flesh and blood?

Then your light will break forth like the dawn, and your healing will quickly appear; then your righteousness will go before you, and the glory of the Lord will be your rear guard. Then you will call, and the Lord will answer; you will cry for help, and he will say: Here am I.

If you will do away with the yoke of oppression, with the pointing finger and malicious talk, and if you spend your-selves on behalf of the hungry and satisfy the needs of the oppressed, then your light will rise in the darkness, and your night will become like the noonday.

If you call the Sabbath a delight and the Lord's holy day honourable, and if you honour it by not going your own way and not doing as you please or speaking idle words, then you will find your joy in the Lord.

———◦———

I don't know if it's because most Westerners considering themselves Christian have never heard God's take on what is and what is not acceptable religion, which is actually no religion at all, or we've somehow misinterpreted or lack the understanding of how to take the ancient words from paper and apply them personally and contemporarily, but it appears as though we may have slept in the days when this message was given.

For many of us, our practical application of God's instruction to protect and rescue the weak consists of dressing up real nice, getting together in a building once a week to sing songs declaring the greatness of God and his grace and mercy, reading a prayer, collecting people's money, and listening to a guy talk about what God really means when he says, *"If you love me, your automatic reaction will be to do the very things that I do, and even more,"* while still accepting as normal our self-centred, self-serving Christian culture. If we would walk in this love, loving others as we are loved, as Jesus said we would (not should), then this is a disturbing indicator that we do not know, and are not subsequently living in his love. When this is the case, we've missed it altogether.

I think the words and stories in the bible are a part of a story that is not meant merely to be known, but to embolden us to live extraordinarily as immortals. Our personal stories, our day-to-day living in God's Love, are a big part of another of God's books—the Book of Life. I think that where the real power lies is in trusting that God's way and his strength will be made perfect in spite of our weakness if we just show up, in spite of any fears. It's called faith, and it's only rewarded when it is exercised and tested by action.

But he said to me, "My grace is sufficient for you, for my power is made perfect in weakness." Therefore I will boast all the more gladly about my weaknesses, so that the power of Jesus may rest on me. (2 Corinthians 12:9)

It makes no sense at all that we would read words intended to strengthen and embolden and encourage and move us, and then just sit on them. It would be like training all our lives for a race that we'll never run. If that's the case, I choose beer, buffalo wings, and a real big TV.

This is how we know what love is: Jesus laid down His life for us. And we ought to lay our lives down for our brothers [each other] . . . let us not love with words or tongue but with actions and in truth. (1 John 3:16, 18)

The reality is that knowing and loving Jesus according to the words of Jesus translates into a heart of compassion towards those around us. Compassion is seeing life through another's eyes.

When I think about a little foreigner kid, someone like my little girls, forced into prostitution, being roughed up and abused by predators, I think, *What if I were that kid, or what if those were my kids?* If I were that kid, I would hope and pray that someone like me would get together with a few friends and come and rescue me. If they were my kids, I would spare no risk, expense, or blood—mine included—in order to rescue them.

And if I were the guy down the street that's been misunderstood most of his life, now in the middle of an ugly divorce—or a widow, an orphan, or someone disabled, and so on—I would hope and pray for a true friend to come into my life and make me family. There is so much hurt and brokenness, and loneliness, and depression right in our neighbourhoods and under our noses; where we work, where we play, right in our churches.

There is no guilt-trip here. Don't just do "it," whatever "it" is, because someone said you're supposed to or because it's the *Christian thing* to do. Jesus doesn't want it that way. He doesn't want *you* that way. He just wants us to know him and experience his love truly and personally. He knows that when a person truly experiences and knows his love and friendship, that person will never fear this world's consequences again.

———◦———

Do not be afraid of those who kill the body but cannot kill the soul. (Matthew 10:28)

———◦———

Once we reconcile what and who Jesus is, in a personal and natural way, rather than simply intellectually or technically, we *will* know him as Lord, he *will* be our friend, and our lives *will* reflect his love.

Parting shot...

A person who has been guaranteed immortality by the one possessing the power to grant it will not live to protect their life, but will live without concern for personal safety, if they truly believe it.

Jesus said that sharing in his life's work would result in immortality, yet people calling themselves Christians today are highly stressed over safety and spend billions of dollars on personal comfort, insurance, and security. This should not be.

If we will make the effort to get to know Jesus intimately and personally, and trust the eternal promise, we are inviting the most radical and rewarding life experiences that anyone could ever know. We will go where few would dare to go, surrounded by a very diverse and unlikely cast of comrades, and we will share in the most awesome friendships and adventure known, this side of heaven.

———◦———

And everyone who has left houses or brothers or sisters or father or mother or children or fields for my sake will receive a hundred times as much and will inherit eternal life (immortality). (Matthew 19:29)

———◦———

"God is preparing His heroes, and when the opportunity comes, he can fit them into their places in a moment. And the world will wonder where they came from." A.B. Simpson

WHAT DO YOU REALLY KNOW?

We know nothing, unless, and until it has been done.

Jesus connected person-to-person and not as an obligatory, or even recommended religious group event or activity of the "church of Galilee." Even while he was a part of a larger group, his interactions generally took on a personal nature.

A new command I give you: Love one another. As I have loved you, so you must love one another. By this all men will know that you are my disciples, if you love one another. (John 13:35)

It is through observation that people will know who the followers of Jesus are by the way and to the degree that they are known to love. We will be seen for what we truly are, and not by verbal professions of faith, but by the way that we actively love as individuals.

Jesus also said, *You are my friends if you do what I command,* which is really no command at all (but a bridge from the law to freedom), when you consider that he also called them friends and not servants performing obligatory duties. What did he *command* then? He commanded us to love each other as he loves us. The foundation of Christian belief and lifestyle is then centred on how it is that we experience the love of Jesus, and what identifies the legitimacy of a follower of Jesus then comes down to how we each follow his example and love others in the same manner.

In his day, rather than being a part of the solution, a spiritually blinded, self-righteous, and compromising, religious elect—hell-bent on retaining their position, and religious control within the status quo—did everything in their power to shut him up and shut him down.

Jesus deliberately and emphatically embraced and exercised meekness, humility, equality, and friendship with the least of the least—widows, divorcees, lepers, prostitutes, thieves, and orphans to name a few. This cannot be emphasized enough. He mended the hearts of the hurting and broken by going to them and befriending them where they were at, an approach that was foreign and actually despised by the leadership of the day.

You don't know what you don't know...

Recently, I was present for a fascinating conversation between my young friend Graham and another one of my friends,

Brent, who's been a police officer for the past twenty-plus years. After making the introduction, they asked what men always ask each other upon meeting: "So what do you do?" When Graham told Brent that he had just finished earning his college degree in criminology and was now looking for work, Brent's eyes lit up.

"So tell me," he asked Graham, "What did you learn? What do you know about crime and criminals? How are you going to deal with a criminal?"

Graham sort of stammered at first, then went on to tell Brent about what he had learned through his textbooks, studies, and lectures. The whole time Brent locked eyes with Graham, not once blinking. When Graham was done telling Brent about all that he knew, Brent took another step closer. With a piercing look in his eyes, and with only a foot between them, Brent calmly and slowly, emphasizing each word, said to him, "You—don't—know—anything. Until you get out there and put those written words to the test, you only have some theory in your head, but you personally don't know anything."

Obviously Graham wasn't going to just settle for that— after all he had just spent the past five years studying his tail off! He tried to make his point incontestably in order to sway Brent's point of view about what he thought he knew, but Brent countered with story after story about experiencing life in the real world of criminology, of criminals up in his face, of rescuing abused women and children, and of holding the hands of comrades as they lay on the pavement dying.

They debated while I refereed for the next hour, but no matter what Brent said to convince Graham that you don't really know anything until you've done it and experienced it firsthand, Graham wouldn't totally believe it. He didn't know what he didn't know, and because he didn't know, he never knew that he didn't know anything. Until he put his feet on the pavement and did what the books said, he never would.

———◦———

Rejoice with those who rejoice; mourn with those who mourn. Live in harmony with one another. Do not be proud. Be willing to associate with people of low position. Don't be conceited. Don't repay anyone evil for evil. (Romans 12:18-20)

———◦———

Your fight is my fight...

Do you know how it feels to hold and love a baby that was thrown away to die in a muddy ditch? Have you wrapped your arms around and kissed the diseased? Have you sat in the dirt with the homeless? If you have never experienced the effect of being broken with the broken, try leaving the confines of comfy, sanitized, trendy, buddy-buddy North American

"Christianity" and spend some quality time with who you know to be hurting and broken, outside of religious events and organizations. It doesn't matter who you are, something happens to you that changes you. It is here that you will know that you are truly alive and that God is alive in you, softening and transforming you from the inside out.

Take a step out of the typical routine and put yourself in a position to spend one-on-one time with the elderly, widows and orphans, the disabled, poverty-stricken, the diseased and dying, then you'll *know* what Jesus is really talking about when he talks about *food* we may currently know nothing about.

Anyone who has faith in me will do what I have been doing. (John 14:12)

Jesus' lifestyle was a model of real life application for those individuals who would choose to "follow" the extremely satisfying, personally sacrificial lifestyle, of committed friendship and devotion, to attain something of greater worth than temporal financial security, a full belly, and a good night's sleep.

Putting personal power and strength under discipline, and to use it to elevate the lowly and stand up to the bully on their behalf without imminent recognition or reward, is the very definition of the meekness that characterized Jesus' approach to living. Intentional or not, this was a leadership style that attracted the humble but repulsed the proud. (I think it was clearly intentional.)

Greater love has no one than this; that he lay down his life for his friends. You are my friends if you do what I command. (John 15:13–14)

Relationship or friendship with Jesus will become something which goes beyond a task or calculated obligatory obedience in any way. Rabbi living out equality and becoming *friend* redefines the role and style of leadership, and develops unity at a whole new personal level. There comes a point when the relationship is no longer about authority and, or obedience but grows in depth; it becomes more a case of "wild horses couldn't keep me away from you and what you got goin' on. Your fight is my fight and there's no place I'd rather be." This was another new perspective that Jesus appeared to clearly imprint on the lives of his followers.

There is a bond that is developed between people, especially when they walk through the fire together, and are tested by some adversity.

My closest and most trusted friends are those people who stood and stand beside me, and walk beside me when life's certainty becomes uncertain, and the calm sea turns violent. They are the people who, when things get tough, choose to stand and fight rather than turn and run away.

When one of the guys on my football team gets drilled, every one of us takes notice of who on the other team was involved and will take every opportunity for the rest of the game to show him what it feels like when you mess with even one of us. We win more than we lose. We are a broken bunch who miss assignments, blow coverages, and throw interceptions, but our team/friendship culture is to pick each other up and do our best together to minimize the consequence of the mistake. Football is just a dumb game but this principal of fighting together develops strength together and confidence as individuals.

———◦———

I have told you this so that my joy may be in you, and that your joy may be complete. (John 15:11)

———◦———

When Jesus says that we should lay down our lives for each other, he's not necessarily talking about dying for someone physically, although that option is always on the table. He's instructing us to leave our old way of thinking and living—our life of self-centred independence and comfort and false security—and in turn reveals to us our true wants and heart's desires. Then he invites us to join a revolution that is about liberating "kids" who have become lost, enslaved, and "orphaned." It may cost us our physical lives—and good for us if it does—but it might not.

We might be faced with something much more difficult than taking a bullet for a stranger, such as an eighty-five-year struggle to resist and overcome the pattern of our self-centred and indulgent living, which has been woven into the fabric of North American society as something we believe we're entitled to.

We may spend eighty-five years having people looking at us through the stereotype of crutch-bearing, weak-minded, and delusional. That stereotype, however, has often been earned, as people who call themselves "freedom fighters" who do little more to fight for the King than dress up real nice, sing songs, and sit through a lecture, during a weekly two-hour exercise we call church, unfortunately leaves little room for debate in the minds of those on the *outside looking in*. I know that may sound a bit harsh but we really need to get our head and heart around the practicality of what we're doing and especially why we're doing.

Laying down our lives like Jesus did is truly sharing our lives in the same manner. We can do no better and we are commanded to do no less. Not a command by a power hungry-tyrant, but more a union with a king who is a friend, sharing his life's passion and "setting the table" for his return to fully and truly liberate.

It is Jesus' love, passion, and personal friendship that will inspire us to enter into a lifestyle that we do not yet fully know, and a lifestyle that will create in us joy, peace, and freedom that we have spent our lives searching for, but have never been able to grasp. His friendship inspires us to step out of our comfort zone and take some chances in order to display abundant life by living an abundant life in and through his, and his in ours.

———◦———

I am in my father, and you are in me and I am in you… he who loves me will be loved by my father, and I too will love him and show myself to him. (John14:20-21)

———◦———

There is nothing symbolic or ritualistic about it, and this is not a symbolic relationship that is characterized by performing habitual rituals. This is either the real deal, or this is completely, one hundred percent bogus. Jesus is not Santa Claus for grownups, even if he does, in fact, know that we're all a bit more naughty than nice. This is about utilizing the life we've been given to the best of our abilities, and our abilities magnify—God alive in us. That's huge!

Great potential...potentially great....

We live in the land of opportunity—opportunity to please ourselves for a temporary existence, or opportunity to lay away treasure in God's eternal kingdom by realizing his love and what we've been given, and doing the best we can with the opportunities presented:

It will be like a man going on a journey, who called his servants and entrusted his property to them. To one he gave five talents of money, to another two talents, and to another one talent, each according to his ability. Then he went on his journey. The man who had received the five talents went at once and put his money to work and gained five more.... (Matthew 25:14–16)

*After a long time, the master of those servants returned and settled accounts with them. The man who had received the five talents brought the other five. "Master," he said, "you entrusted me with five talents. See, I have gained five more." His master replied, "Well done, good and faithful servant! You have been faithful with a few things; I will put you in charge of many things. Come and share your master's happiness." *(Matthew 25:19–21)

This was the master's take on how to reward those who had been given much and did what they could with what they were given. On the other hand, take a look at what Jesus says to the guy who was given one talent and did nothing with it:

Take the talent from him and give it to the one who has ten talents. For everyone who has will be given more, and he will have an abundance. Whoever does not have, even what he has will be taken from him. Oh, and throw that worthless servant outside, into the darkness, where there will be weeping and gnashing of teeth. (Matthew 25:28–30)

Just imagine how the Master would feel towards servants who were given five talents and used them to buy unnecessary stuff and comfort for themselves, and only kicked back ten percent. At least the dude with two gave back two. As a man who has been entrusted with much, I find that to be a very sobering thought.

Do you not know that in a race all the runners run, but only one gets the prize? Run in such a way as to get that prize. (1Cor9:24)

Parting Shot...

Following Jesus is an individual pursuit. Many people share their frustration and confusion with me of how a close friendship with Jesus eludes them. As helpful as a church service can be, by itself it has actually proven to stymy and stunt personal spiritual maturity when *relational pursuit* becomes corporate *spiritual management*. We can't get to know Jesus personally, and in depth, in a church or in a group setting any more than we can a future spouse or even a good friend. It comes down to personal desire, personal pursuit, and personal discovery, which leads to camaraderie and a feeling of unity and oneness.

Personally investing in a friendship with Jesus is how that deep personal intimacy is developed, and is also how a person invests for the future; no one else can invest for us. Talking about investing does not put money in the bank and food on the table. But again, it is a no-brainer. If we personally know and love Jesus, it is evidenced naturally by how we look at and actively love those in our world. No guilt, no manipulation, no coercion, we are what we are.

--------◇--------

If anyone obeys his words, God's love is truly made complete in him. This is how we know we are in him: Whoever claims to live in him must walk as Jesus did. (1 John 2:4-6)

--------◇--------

What is it, then, to walk like Jesus walked in today's culture? What does that look like? That's the question that every person needs to work out personally by knowing firsthand how Jesus walked. How is he walking with you? How would you like him to walk with you?

--------◇--------

Remain in me, and I will remain in you. (John15:4)

--------◇--------

PLAYING THE ODD(BALL)S

I ran into a friend recently who, after being involved in a car accident a few years ago, was paralyzed from the waist down. I hadn't seen her or her husband for a couple years at least and was a bit curious as to how they had adjusted to the obvious changes. I didn't ask too many questions because I really didn't know what to say or how to say it, but I noticed she didn't smile as much as before and she seemed a bit sad. I couldn't blame her. I can't remotely imagine what it must be like to go from walking, running, playing ball on Saturday, and on Sunday being confined to a wheelchair for the rest of my life. I don't have a second thought when it comes to enjoying my mobility from day to day. Like getting in my truck, paddling a canoe, or going fishing, but all that would change drastically.

Just as I was about to leave, she said to me, "You probably don't know this—not many people do—but Glen (her husband, not his real name) moved out a while ago."

I looked at her, then looked away, then looked at her again. Fighting back tears, when I saw her tears, all I could say was, "I didn't know, I'm really sorry."

I could hardly believe it. The Glen I thought I knew was a God-fearing, family-loving man. I figured he would be the hero and protector and lover of his family, not the guy who hooked up with another woman, and walked away from his disabled wife and daughters. But you know what rocked me the most? I wondered about myself. If my road got really tough, would I stay the course, or would I just walk away too? What was the foundation of my life really built on? What was truly holding me together? What am I truly made of? Could I weather a storm like theirs?

I wondered about the love I possessed. Was it just a *happy, feel good theory* that I had knowledge of; something that worked for me when life was easy? Do I just possess a self-serving, tit-for-tat sort of love, or do I truly know and function in the protecting love and compassion that Jesus spoke of, as my default position?

We hear the word *love* being thrown around all the time, but what is *love* according to Jesus? Who is my neighbor that Jesus would like to love through me? What does that look like practically? We'll know that once we realize the Father's love for us as individuals.

He cares for scumbags while they're still scumbags. He cares for jerks while they're still jerks. He cares for adulterers while they're still adulterers. He cares for crooks while they're still crooks. He cares for you and me, and wants the best for us, even when we aren't thinking about him, even when we think we want nothing to do with him at all. This is the model of God Love—*agape* love—period. It is not for the weak-willed or the faint of heart, because it thrives on fighting against the odds.

———

My righteous one will live by faith. And if he shrinks back, I will not be pleased with him. But we are not of those who shrink back and are destroyed, but of those who believe and are saved. (Hebrews 10:38–39)

———

Legitimately Steve...

Let me tell you a story about my friend Steve. Not long ago I was a pretty competitive guy with a similar outlook to winning as Lombardi when he said: "Winning isn't everything, it's the only thing." One Sunday afternoon we got all the boys (and Kelsey) together and went out to play some pick-up football. When we got to the field my buddy Darren met us with a few guys from his church in the city.

One of those guys was named Steve. Steve was a software designer, 135 lbs, complete with a pair of glasses and a polo shirt with a sewn in pocket. It didn't take long to see that

Steve hadn't played much football. In fact, Steve had never played football before and wouldn't you know it, somehow Steve made his way onto my team.

Since I was the oldest one out there and had a bit of a role model responsibility, I didn't say anything audibly, but my body-language said it all I'm sure. On the inside I was definitely pouty and totally deflated; *"may as well go home, this was going to be a disaster"*. Judging by the warm-up, I didn't think Steve was even capable of catching a cold that day. I think they got up on us two scores early and I was hoping someone would soon offer up a mercy trade in order to deliver me from this losing feeling and the *loser* hell that I found myself.

They were up a couple scores and after their latest score they kicked it off to us and the ball bounced way behind everyone down into our end zone. No one said anything out loud, and I thought we were pretty much conceding a touchback when Steve picked up the ball and walked out of the end zone with it. He walked up to the ten yard line, then the twenty, and by the time he had walked past the thirty we all just assumed he didn't know where the line of scrimmage was. All of a sudden he quickly looked around and saw no one near him and sprinted for their end zone. It was a touchdown! We all had a bit of a laugh about it but no one contested the fact that it was a legit touchdown, and Steve scored it, all by himself.

We grabbed him and shook him and congratulated him, knocking his glasses off in the process. He was totally stoked. We kicked back to them and somehow stopped them from scoring.

When we got the ball back we noticed that they were doubling our best receiver, leaving Steve basically uncovered, so on a wing and a prayer we threw to Steve, and Steve somehow caught it, and he ran and we blocked and Steve scored again. As the game progressed, Steve became a new man, a warrior, half man-half *beast*. His shirt had been torn good on one play so he tore it the rest of the way and wore it as a Samurai headband, so the rest of the team took ours off too except for Kelsey. (Yeah, I got the girl on my team too!)

On one play Steve got totally creamed and broke his glasses and cut his nose but he fought all the more. With half vision, half naked, and a bloodied nose, we threw to Steve and Steve caught it and Steve scored again...a deflected pass caught...touchdown, again. The guy could run like a rabbit!

In the end, while the best athlete (Sorry Kelsey, that would be me, it's my book!) on the team was pouting, the one with what appeared to be the least ability, seized his opportunity, gave it all he had, and won the game for his team. I learned a valuable lesson about how Father God's plan very much includes winning with what may be *perceived* as less, on paper. I also learned what made a valuable teammate, valuable.

Less is more...

I have learned that I am never more satisfied than when I start with and succeed with less. It is also extremely satisfying to watch and be a part of someone's personal transformation. We do, however, need to show up and play regardless of how things appear *on paper*, regardless of *the odds*, if we're ever going to share in life's most satisfying victories.

We can do this. A story about coming back against the odds strikes a nerve in all of us. Deep down, we want to live like this, and we can make this our lifestyle. Once it is tasted, this *winning with less* business is totally satisfying.

———◦———

… anyone who is not willing to give up his very life—he cannot be my disciple. (Luke14:26-27)… any of you who does not give up everything he has cannot be my disciple. (Luke 14:33)

———◦———

Demonstrating this powerful lifestyle of redemption and laying down of one's own life, doesn't always have to look like a big, dramatic production. In fact, often it's with the most gentle, subtle, personal gestures that yield the greatest impact. We are especially impacted when doing so, moves us out of our comfort zone.

At times it would be easy to hear the message of this book as sounding like the focus is all about doing. I want to take a moment here to confirm that is not the case. This abundant life really begins as a state of *being*. It is about being in the presence and love of the father, and it is about remaining in that love, and transformation which occurs as a result. Only love can transform another heart to love. It can't be scared in, or manipulated in, commanded in, or forced in. Love breeds love, nothing else can. This is where everything begins. It's also where everything completes. This is the Father's plan to reconcile and return peace to his creation. If the plan works, and I think it will, one day we won't even call love, love; we'll call it normal.

When a lady is proposed to and she gets that ring on her finger that she was longing for, she has a *fresh* sense of knowing that she is the object of great affection, that she is wanted, that she is loved, and she is radiant. She is the most beautiful person to be around and nothing around her seems to faze this beautiful spirit that she possesses when this love is known and lived in, and fresh.

This is what I'm talking about. It is walking regularly in the love of the Father which will keep us *fresh* when we are aligned with him and our lives remain centered on his acceptance and approval, regardless of our human weaknesses. This develops personal confidence, with confidence we step out, and whether we win, lose, or draw, faith is developed so we do it again and again, pushing our boundaries.

I married a girl who was perceived to be an extremely shy introvert. When we first started dating, I could tell that she always wanted to be with me and do things with me, but I always had to take the conversational lead. Drawing out a conversation with her was like pulling hens' teeth, which isn't done much anymore, but I've been told is very difficult.

Even now she's still a bit nervous when venturing out for a first encounter with someone she doesn't know, but she has experienced firsthand that there are great spiritual and relational rewards attached when she, in spite of her fears, dares to initiate, unconditional of a potentially awkward or negative reception.

Not that long ago, while doing some contract work, I ran into a lady who had been in our country for only two days. She had a four-year-old and a six-month-old baby and had no vehicle available during the day because her husband had it at work.

I knew I should do something to help her out, but for the life of me I really didn't know how to appropriately handle this one myself. Knowing full well that this would be a stretch for my wife, I phoned Dana and asked her if she would be willing to meet this lady and take her shopping and show her around the area.

Dana readily agreed, and with no formal introduction, and just my vague directions to her house, they met up and did what most women do very well: they went shopping. Usually this is where our self-designed random acts of kindness begin and end, but not when our Father is the architect.

Out of this seemingly random encounter, family friendships have been forged, meals have been shared, and we men protect each other weekly on the football field. How did it happen? Because Dana, the individual, stepped a bit out of her comfort zone and met a stranger. In spite of her initial fear, her confidence in the love the Father has for her, was the confidence that moved her. She had nothing to lose, and everything to gain.

"Perfect love drives out fear." Why? We've all heard it said that love is blind. This is especially true with the love that defines God. God's love drives one to act, regardless of fear, as the power of his love simply over-rides any other consideration; it is a little *stupid* or *blind* to natural obstructions or fears. When *love comes to town,* fear is nullified, and action is the result. This is the working out of faith.

Parting Shot...

It is very difficult to embark upon a lifestyle that is lived out against the odds, and with reckless abandon, but I can promise you that there is nothing more rewarding than winning when it feels like the deck is stacked against you. This is the reality of the faith that we profess. One man stood up to a jaded world and misdirected religious culture alone, with no army and no weapon other than love, with his greatest companion being the confidence of being loved perfectly, and knowing unity with his Father at all times.

I cannot overstate that just doing nice things for people in order to gain a temporary moment or two of feeling good isn't the objective, because that in itself is self-centred and not satisfying, and we will not find what we truly are looking for.

The point and source of satisfaction is found in the relationship of a child walking with his or her Father in unity. We win by being with him, and not in doing the things we think he wants apart from him. The Father's got this. He doesn't need us, but he wants us. He wants us with him, doing things with him, because we have affection for him, because we know and trust his love and affection for us.

It's time we slow things down and listen for the *voice of truth*. God's Spirit will give us the insight and courage to step into unchartered territory, to face giants, to fight great armies, and to love our wives and kids, friends, neighbors, and strangers, together in step with him. That is the mission. It is often walked out in the dark—by feel, by trust, and by faith. It is the walking with and rescuing of the desperate and hopeless with our Father. It is selfless, it is against the odds, and it is a *rush*.

THE HEART OF THE MATTER

We are physical and spiritual beings. The flesh will deteriorate and eventually turn to dust, but the spirit will live forever. It is for this reason that although we live in this world, it is not our long-term future, and we must not be duped into simply accepting a lifestyle of short-term thinking.

We need to be aware of and defend ourselves against the short-sighted traps of consumerism and acquisitions, investing in, and living for physical comfort and the insatiable pleasures of this world, and tit-for-tat relational interaction. They are working in total opposition to what Jesus defines as the means for spiritual investing in God's kingdom.

Do not store up for yourselves treasures on earth where moth and rust destroy and where thieves break in and steal, but store up for yourselves treasure in heaven . . .

for where your treasure is, there your heart will be also.
(Matthew 6:19–21)

———◦———

So how's it going? Where is the heart at these days? Are we storing up wealth here on this earth, or are we storing up wealth in heaven? If we're storing up wealth in heaven, what is it? What does it look like? Ever really thought about it much? Or is this talk about storing up wealth in heaven nothing more than religious jargon or some mysterious metaphor?

Let's take a step back to *"where your treasure is, there your heart will be also."* We need to ask ourselves: What is our treasure? What do we really value most? Where is our heart at? What do we really want? What do we think of when we read the following verse?

———◦———

Your kingdom come and your will be done on earth as it is in heaven. (Matthew 6:10)

———◦———

God's kingdom come...is that what we really want? Really? What are we prepared to do in order to truly be about God's kingdom flourishing on earth as it is in Heaven? How far would we go in order for all relationships to be reconciled? That is God's ultimate desire, and it sure seems like from everything we've covered so far, people are what he treasures most.

If we were to be able to strip away all the layers of what it is that we think we want in and out this life; personal worth, unconditional acceptance, and peace, is what the *human machine* covets most, and it is exactly what our Father wants to give to us, and out through us.

I have told you these things, so that in me you may have peace. In this world you will face troubles. But take heart, I have overcome the world. (John16:33)

Redemption...

One of the best love story movies that I still watch at least once a year is the modern western classic, *Tombstone*. I am just about brought to tears every time I watch that movie.

I especially love the part when after Wyatt Earp's brother, Morgan, is killed by the cowboys, Wyatt takes matters into his own hands and, with just a few friends, attempts to rid the earth of this ruthless gang of thugs. Towards the end of the movie, the odds are stacked against Wyatt and his few fighting friends. The cowboys have all their men together and look primed to take out Wyatt and his few loyal men.

Johnny Ringo is supposed to be the best gunslinger around, and earlier in the movie, challenged Wyatt to a duel. Wyatt cannot say no to this challenge, because guys like him never back down from bullies. However, he knows he can't win, because he's never had a real quick hand as a gunfighter. The only real gunfighter they have is Doc Holiday, but he's sick in bed and looks to be dying with tuberculosis.

As Wyatt gets close to the big oak tree where the battle is to take place, he hears gunshots from the area and rushes in to see what was going on. When he gets there he finds his buddy, Doc Holiday, standing over the dead body of Johnny Ringo.

To have Doc Holiday, who on paper would appear to be less-than-reliable, and a highly unlikely friend, show up—even though he was deathly sick—to fight Johnny Ringo in Wyatt's place, rocks me every time I watch it. You really can't judge a book by its cover. People and circumstances are seldom what they appear, good or bad.

This is a story about redemption across the board. Wyatt has a death-wish as he reconciles the death of his younger brother, as his fault. When it comes time to die, though, and he then realizes in that moment, that he really doesn't want to die, he's out of options. He's as good as dead. Nothing can save him now…he knows it in his heart. Then somehow, someone…stands in his place and fights his fight, without him even asking, and solves his quandary for him. A miracle…. Friendship at its pinnacle; when it seemed impossible.

It touches the heart like nothing else. It's about a friend who stands in our place. It's about using our lives to bring something of substance into others' lives, to lay it all down for the good of another. This is the love possessed by one and given for another that changes the heart of both the giver and receiver.

I'm quite confident in saying that the soul of a human being is in fact the treasure of God's Kingdom that Jesus speaks of, and love and friendship are how we invest in the re-building of God's family.

Treasure in heaven...

While a woman may be our wife, she is first Jesus's sister and friend, and we need to protect and build her up first and foremost because we love him; in turn we must love her so that we may share a part of her ultimate perfection and potential by his design. That is also how we need to see our daughters, sons, our neighbours, and neighbour's daughters and sons. This is our role. This is storing up treasure in heaven.

Jesus said in Matthew 5 that the meek would inherit the earth. Personally, I would be happy to just inherit a good fishing lake somewhere in the Rockies, or even a little piece of coastline somewhere in the South Pacific. If God insists, though, I'll take the earth, but until then, I have some responsibility's to attend to.

I would love to be meek. To be meek is first to have confidence, so that we can humble ourselves, and then use the ability or abilities we are given to come beneath someone and lift them up, while attempting to remain invisible in the process. It is a power not used for self-serving ambition but power under control. That is almost God-like, and a very useful attribute.

This begs the question: How seriously do we take what Jesus said? Was he just thinking out loud, making small talk and making random suggestions, or was he spelling out the what, how, and why of God's plan and purpose, and our role as we participate within it?

According to Jesus, if we love him and love God, we have our priorities set on his priorities. He in turn will reward us by giving to us the true desires of our heart—personal harmony. This is what we've been longing for and missing since the curse of death was imposed and conveyed through the story of Adam and Eve, choosing to know both good and evil over trusted friendship with God.

Each one of us should test our own actions ... without comparing ourselves to anyone else... (Gal6:4)

If we will trust Jesus and take this all the way, there is a great possibility that our lives will become seasoned with spontaneous adventures and fresh and diverse personal encounters.

Engagement...

It starts with knowing the love, mercy, and compassion Father God has for us. This leads to desiring to know God better, and as we experience more of God's love, we find ourselves developing more grace and compassion for others. Jesus indicated that this is tangibly and naturally accomplished as we love our neighbour by putting ourselves in someone else's shoes, doing to them and for them what we would hope for ourselves. It sounds a lot to me like what Jesus is talking about is simply old-school friendship.

I was hungry, and I was thirsty; I was a stranger; I needed clothes; I was sick; I was imprisoned . . . and either you did or did not look after [them] me. (My paraphrase of Matthew 25:35–45)

Who is Jesus to me? Is it safe to say that Jesus displayed great personal affection for the un-popular and the hurting, and shameful people of his day? Would we then not also have affection for people regardless of superficial blemishes or behaviours, similar to the affection he has for me? Would we not see value in the life of a beggar? Would not the investing in the lives of people be a higher priority than anything else? I not only believe this to be true, I would go so far as to say that according to the words that Jesus spoke, along with the life he lived, it is absolutely true. At least that's what he said that friends of his would be about.

Do you know that a human being dies from starvation about every seven seconds? Did you also know that there is enough food produced to feed the global population twice over? My daughter told me that the other day. That's a real shame.

Did you know there are over two billion professing Christians in the world, with two hundred and forty million of them living in North America alone?

Do you know what an army of two hundred million lovers of people with cash in their pockets could accomplish if they were united by God's Spirit and living for his kingdom and not their own?

Do you know what one person can do in the life of a lonely person if their eyes were opened to see them?

From time to time people will ask me where all the lonely and broken people are. Not seeing them around is a sign that one needs to get out more, because when living where God's kingdom is most active, they are everywhere.

The accounting...

If we want to end any speculation and know exactly where we stand and where the heart is at, take a good look at what we've collected around us. Take a good look at how our time is spent, with whom, and for what purpose. Where are my resources going? Where is the money spent? If we will answer those questions honestly, it will be clear where our priorities lie; who we love and serve, and which kingdom we're investing in.

Is this kingdom of God some faraway place somewhere off in the distance? No, it's within us and around us. It is life, participated, with an inclusive and eternal family with a Father, and siblings, who are also friends.

Once, having been asked by the Pharisees when the kingdom of God would come, Jesus replied, "The kingdom of God does not come with your careful observation, nor will people say, 'here it is,' or 'there it is,' because the kingdom of God is within you." (Luke 17:20–21)

The kingdom of God is now within us—it is a kingdom made visible by Gods Spirit, with an agenda, priorities, and even currency. It is where and how we make our stand for living a full and purposeful life today through personal interaction. It is also where and how we store up lasting reward in this life and the life to come.

By the ways of our Father, and life in his kingdom, we are being changed. Becoming more compassionate, becoming a little more meek as we reflect how we are loved, willingly humbling ourselves, knowing this love, and by it—injecting life into others.

Loving others often changes us, as much or more than it changes the people we are directed to love. It is very much a God-like characteristic to be able to give generously, and freely, with no thought of reciprocation. This is the transformation which is truly at the *heart* of the matter.

Parting Shot...

Success in God's kingdom revolves around his love. His love known and experienced personally, moves us, providing courage and confidence and the other necessary tools required to demonstrate his love naturally in all aspects of everyday living.

The entire law is summed up in a single command: Love your neighbor as yourself. If you keep on biting and devouring each other, watch out or you will be destroyed by each other: so I say, live by the Spirit, and you will not gratify the desires of the sinful nature. (Gal5:14-16)

The carnal mind, flesh, or the physical senses are often gratified by *feeling* successful by the man-made standards of this earthly kingdom. If I rely on my senses, I'm thinking primarily of self-preservation. If I'm the one at the top of the food chain, then I might help someone out as long as the calculation works for me. If it makes me feel good, if I get a bit of recognition and applause from my peers, as they remember who *Mr. Good Guy* is and who's on top, and I'm owed a favor in the process.

When you look at the carnal mind and the Spirit side by side, it's quite obvious why Paul said they are in opposition with each other. Which will we choose—self-preservation, or the restoration of others by selflessness? Which would we choose on our own? What it comes down to is this: we are either into God's plan, God's way, all the way, or we are not. This is what Jesus is saying when he says that *we can't serve two masters (Matthew 6:24)*.

I believe God's hope is that every gift, hardship, or blessing, would be used to win back the hearts of his children. When we simply go along with Father's plan, by belief, faith, trust, and friendship; this is more personal communion between you than any form of sacrament. This is worship of the Father in spirit and in authenticity (truth). This is what a Father loves more than anything else, and it is only achieved by following Jesus' example. Love breeds love. Nothing else can.

LESS IS MORE, (MORE OR LESS)

"Real community happens not by fighting for our preferences but in laying down our lives and creating safe places for people to come and be exactly who they are and what they are. We try to maintain a slick and efficient operation, but love, according to Jesus, is not efficient." Wayne Jacobsen

This chapter has proven to be much more difficult to write than any other. I would prefer to speak directly to individuals, friends, and not even touch the subject of "church", collectively, but church reform is clearly the elephant in the room these days. I hope this chapter will not sound critical in the process of identifying any shortcomings, but rather constructive in moving forward with how we may improve.

Further complicating matters for me personally and to which you may relate, is that on one hand, I have a bit of a traditional and sentimental side to me which likes the idea of preserving some forms of useful tradition, but on the other hand, when a tradition has misrepresented its intended purpose and often appears to be causing more damage than good; to me, it's a no-brainer: shake it off, cut it loose, start fresh.

I have made you known to them, and will continue to make you known in order that the love you have for me may be in them and that I myself may be in them. (John17:26)

The traditionally organized church is inadvertently enabling the problem that is the traditionally organized church. What it is unwittingly doing is stymying the transformation, or growth of the individual by creating the illusion that knowing the *Truth* and hearing the *Word* happens primarily at a service or event, by the speaking of words and the hearing of truths. We believe that the words of God spoken by men and women can *fix* us; the words can't and neither can the people. They can only direct us to the One who can give us life; God, the Word (the Father, Jesus, The Spirit).

We also believe that the prayers of "professionals" would somehow possess more *lightning* and be more effective in communicating with our Father than ours would. They don't. Others don't talk to the Father on our behalf any better than we could. In fact, speaking to the Father through a go-between would actually be a bit insulting to our Father I would think. He wants to hear from us directly and we need to hear from Him directly.

This is known as a personal relationship. No one can do this for us, and when we make a habit of having someone else try to do it for us, eventually all meaningful and personal communication is lost. This *thing* between us and God needs to be treated as a deep personal relationship, (son-ship, daughter-ship, friendship), otherwise simply going through religious motions will have us feeling like we're chasing our tails and feeling like we're getting nowhere.

Do you know what the biggest complaint people share with me is in regards to their spiritual lives? They're jumping through all the *right* hoops, yet feel like they're getting nowhere.

Just one...

Your Father in heaven is not willing that any one of these little ones should be lost. (Matt18:14)

Those of us living here in the west, often think that bigger and newer and more, translates into success. In Gods kingdom, that is not so; Jesus says that success is a widow who drops everything to diligently clean out her entire house in order to find one lost coin. (Luke 15:8-10)

Of a shepherd who drops everything and leaves a flock of ninety-nine to go find that one lost sheep wandering alone and in danger. (Luke 15:2-7)

Or a man who discovers one fine pearl and sells everything he once possessed to acquire this one pearl. (Matt 13:44-46)

It's a message of man's need to forego the substituted kingdom he's made for himself in order to rediscover fulfillment and satisfaction in the kingdom God designed for him from the beginning. It's really a message of "less is often more", and "quality is superior to quantity", and that a "quantity of quality" is no more significant, and has no more value than individual quality.

⎯⎯⎯◦⎯⎯⎯

Do not merely listen to the words, and so deceive yourself. Do what it says. (James 1:22)

⎯⎯⎯◦⎯⎯⎯

We've heard these bible stories over and over again from every angle and interpretation under the sun, but what have we really learned by gaining this knowledge? We have dug into the Greek to find true meaning that will suit our circumstance, and have studied hermeneutics to apply these timeless truths to uncover the exact context for which they were written. While staring at and dissecting details and *languages*, we've missed the message.

———◦———

The teachers of the law muttered: This man (Jesus) welcomes sinners and eats with them. (Luke15:2)

———◦———

We've become experts in the law and have alienated the "pagans", and when they do dare to wander onto our turf they leave as confused as ever, because they don't have a clue what it is that we're even talking about. They see no evidence of this truth because we go no further than talking about it—and from fifty feet away.

———◦———

You have insulted the poor. (James2:6) If you show favoritism, you sin and are convicted by the (new) law as lawbreakers.(James2:9)

———◦———

When was the last time we befriended, really befriended, someone from a very different economic bracket, or someone from society's *fringes*? I'm not talking about befriending them by giving them some spare change for a cup of coffee, or generically handing them a plate of food at an inner-city soup kitchen (although that is a great place to get started on the road of personal responsibility and personal friendship).

When was the last time we noticed a lonely person in our church fellowship and invited them over for lunch even once? Or are we too busy lunching with the comfortable, and hanging out with our idea of the cool kids and the shiny folks? Don't deny it cool kids; I know, I was a cool kid. How do you think it's going to feel to be called "not cool" by someone who's not a cool kid anymore? Watch for it, it's coming.

Meanwhile, we gather in our small, medium, and large groups and drink coffee. While the peasants are starving, we're actually telling them to just eat cake, while we pat ourselves on the back and applaud each other for thinking we have an understanding and sometimes profound insight into what we think Paul *really* meant, or what Jesus *really* meant.

Meanwhile, what Jesus *really* meant was what Jesus *really* said and *really* did. It doesn't need to be broken down more than this if we really care to understand: just love your damn neighbour; really. Who is my neighbor? Ever read the story of the good Samaritan? The cross bred Samaritan "dog", he's your neighbor, and you're his.

Cool...

Everyone has heard John 3:16, but I wonder how many people even know that there is a 1 John 3:16. John 3:16 says that whoever *believes*, while 1 John 3:16 identifies and defines *believe:*

This is how we know what love is: Jesus laid down his life for us. And we ought to lay down our lives for others. If anyone has material possessions and sees someone in need but has no pity on him, how can the love of God be in him? Dear children, let us not love with words or tongue, but in actions and in truth. (1 John 3:16)

This is the point. All of the bible is simply stories within a greater story of who God is, how badly he wants us to be in good fellowship with him, how we walk away, and the way back to him. A theological debate is not required if we would just take a few steps back and simplify things.

These are not difficult concepts to understand, but are impossible concepts to live out as long as we choose to try to keep up our love affair with the self-fueled ways of the world system, and settle for a hybrid-version of religious gathering that has become our norm. We are not cool kids, so we can stop trying to act like we are, because not-cool trying to look cool, looks really uncool.

Cool and relevant is not our goal or means to being attractive to a broken and hurting world. The way we love the world (1 John 3:16) as the Father loves us, and others, is the light in the darkness (John1:5). That is attractive. Take religion out of it, and it's almost irresistible. Now that's cool.

I have never been dissed or ridiculed by loving someone with zero conditions or strings attached, by not judging them or feeling a need to point out what might be clear behavioural improvements. In our Western culture, *God love* is not ridiculed, it is coveted.

The church does not need any more *great minds* to help us understand this better. We already have access to millions of highly informative podcasts by gifted speakers, yet people are still leaving the traditional church culture in droves; over 3000 daily. Why do you think that is?

Many of those who are leaving and those who have left understand just fine. That's actually why many are leaving. The people who are really looking are seeing clearly and understand that the equation that's being taught in the *classroom* and witnessed inside...doesn't work outside in the real world.

They understand that the way to the heart of the matters that please God most is not through regular attendance, picketing, and petition; but of grace, compassion, and committed friendship. They are leaving the house each day to be just that, but more practically and naturally, in every-day life.

They understand that it's not by human might that things will be made right, but by God's Spirit and God's love. They understand that we are strangers and aliens and that this is not our final destination. They know not to put eternal hope in this kingdom, and so they don't fight over the things that are typically fought over in this world.

Jesus wants to work with people who will truly love his Father and love his plan with all their hearts. They are his friends, and they will gladly do anything he's involved in, because that's what friends do. The church that Jesus is building is being built by and with friends of Jesus who both know and will be involved in the Father's business, the Father's *Way*. That's what this all is about. The *way* back home to Father.

———◦———

I no longer call you servants, because a servant does not know his master's business. Instead, I have called you friends, for everything that I learned from my Father I have made known to you . . . this is my command: Love each other. (John 15:15 and 17)

———◦———

My wife and I have been married now for 24 years. Not a bad start, but we have a long way to go. I didn't marry my wife because I loved her—I initially married her because I loved *me*. I loved the way she made me feel. I loved what she did for me. I loved the way she looked. I loved the way she adored everything about me.

I had no idea what it meant to love, and I took her for granted for years. I know at times I still do, but I'm learning. After twenty-some years now, I'm starting to see that it is my protecting her and sacrificing for her that is leading me to value her beyond what I ever understood before. The more that I invest into her personally and our relationship, the more value the relationship has to me.

The more that I invest into her, the more she realizes her value, by being loved, and she lives out of that love towards me and to our children and to the friends of our children. God love feeds off of itself to produce more love that is fed off of. This is how a positive cultural shift can take place, slowly but effectively, just about anywhere.

The funny thing about it is that it was her consistent love for me that made me see my lack of love for her in the first place. If I would not have matured from what initially drew me to my wife (her love for me), I have no doubt that we would have been divorced long ago. We've never attended a marriage enrichment conference and have no marriage strategy other than personally getting to know what Jesus said, and pursuing spiritual oneness with Jesus and Father God through open and honest personal dialogue, bringing us into his love together. Oddly enough, it appears that this is also the picture of the church and how Jesus is building his.

———◦———

Matt16:24 "If anyone would come after me he must deny himself and take up his cross and follow me."

———◦———

If you are married it starts right there, if you are single it starts with the people in your apartment complex. Just take an interest and invest in whoever winds up in front of you. There's a good chance Father put them there.

Jesus spelled it out very clearly that a lifestyle of *God-Love* is the leadership plan in his kingdom. That might begin in a church building as it did with me, but it won't mature *there*. Ninety-five percent of the "the plan" is made effective through personal friendship and sacrifice in natural, daily living.

Sacrificing of self is the key that unlocks the door of friendship and brings with it peace and joy. No one can say enough and, or do this for us. We, however, have become accustomed to hearing the theological truth from others and have never experienced nor been taught practically by a healthy combination of words and experience, and have now mistakenly replaced a vibrant and active, life-changing response, with intellectual acknowledgement. In other words: We may have become a bunch of theologically saturated, calculating "servants" who have become well trained at hearing and talking about a faith that the evidence would suggest we may not ourselves possess.

That thought rocks me to the core, but the evidence to support it is overwhelming. Millions of dollars are being spent annually by the traditional church big-wigs on conferences with clever names like *Exponential* and *Disciple-shift*, because it is crystal clear that the traditional style of doing church in North America is not even remotely healthy and vibrant and growing fruit.

Jesus said that he would build his church, and he is— and it is slowly moving out from every nook and cranny imaginable. A lover here and a lover there, touching and moving and intertwining and intersecting lives all over this planet as he and his friends hold onto the things of this world loosely and simply do what comes naturally by remaining in his love.

We who would consider ourselves as leaders have invited the responsibility of walking this message out. We may be called preachers or teachers, but this does not make us exempt from doing all that Jesus says about loving our neighbour. In fact, if and when we understand the very "talks" and messages we're giving to others, it would become quite obvious.

————⊙————

I beat my body and make it my slave so that after I have preached to others, I myself will not be disqualified for the prize. (1Cor9:27)

————⊙————

If we will change our ways and turn back to knowing the Father and his heart, and learn to serve unconditionally in the love of the Father—outside of the boxes that we've created— we will get beyond talking and will walk beside, and show, brothers and sisters the *way*. Then the consumer church will be stripped of its power and influence, and the power of God, made perfect in weakness, will once again rule in the church.

When the Spirit of God and "God Love" is truly invited back into our lives, consumerism will go back the same way it came, along with the unbelief that brought it into the church in the first place. Churches will once again be churches: unsafe gatherings of loved and diverse people who find and love and befriend anyone and everyone, no matter the cost. Business will do what it does, but the two should have never met. Church will cease being a place where we go, and service will not be a thing we perform; it will be a way of life for those who were once dying in a world system of reward for performance.

Jesus consistently directs his followers to display that people are of great value, and the way we live towards them will prove to them that we believe it's true. I believe this with all my heart. I'm certain that we can become the body that Paul describes, having different parts; bones and ligaments and tissue all working together selflessly to bring about the plan of our Father, on this earth in the way that Jesus prayed—loving and caring for each other with an unnatural abandonment to self, loving generously in a way that the people of this world have rarely experienced.

Parting Shot...

As I walk, watch, and pray, when it comes to *Christian service*, something in my gut is telling me that we have the cart ahead of the horse. The lack of attachment, person to person, even during the process of completing *kingdom tasks* together is even a bit bizarre considering Jesus' example.

In a similar way to how our four year-olds are to us, Father truly needs nothing from us. He simply wants us. He is jealous for the relationship with us, of a father's love and a child's trust. I think we will learn and accomplish more by simply living in that relationship, and by walking it out with those who may think they're random strangers but who we see as friends.

We need to return to the one who initiated this Love to be reminded over and again who we are to him, and when we know that, we will naturally look like and be whatever that is. Simply living in God's love and realizing our worth is the greatest gift we could ever possess—one that would be obvious to give away. This is the risk, the adventure, and the plan. And it's a perfect one.

"He is no fool who gives what he cannot keep
to gain what he cannot lose."
Jim Elliot

ALL MY HEART

So many times I've wanted to know and experience more of God; something more personal, something deeper. I'm not sure if it's because I stumble across certain passages or if it's because I'm longing for more that I look for certain passages, but whichever came first, certain passages convince me that—there is more—if I could just reach a bit further, and grasp a little more understanding.

———❖———

"You will look for me and find me when you look for me with all your heart." (Jer29:13)

———❖———

I would love to personally be able to better wrap my head around what "all my heart" even looks like. Don't get me wrong, I've worked pretty hard at times in order to get what I thought I wanted, but I don't know if I've ever committed to doing much of anything in this lifetime with *all* my heart.

Whatever it is that leads a person to ask God to show them what it means to look for him with all their heart, somehow also invites God to show a person more of what's actually on his heart. The closer we get to the heart of the matter, Father shows us more clearly his hearts obsession. Walking *with* God, and looking for him with all our heart takes us to his favorite places. I have discovered repeatedly that his favorite places are the hearts of his children, especially those who are broken and are searching for him.

By simply spending time with our Father, looking for more of him, while obsessing less over our own faults and failures, we begin to get glimpses through his eyes of what he values and what he loves most. Having been given his Spirit as a comforter, guide, and counselor, we can observe by less obstructed sight lines, more of his wisdom, compassion, and the love he has for the people in the world around us.

When we in turn share his love, acceptance, and compassion freely with others, emptying ourselves on and for what and who he loves most, it first affects, and with consistency it begins to infect... and it infects some more. Who it affects, and infects most is what we may find somewhat surprising. Too often we think that living in the Father's love and loving others by it is a tool meant to be effective in changing the hearts of others, and often we're disappointed when we don't see immediate transformation in others. I think we have placed our expectations where they don't belong. I think loving, by design, does more initially for the giver than it does for the one we always thought was on the receiving end.

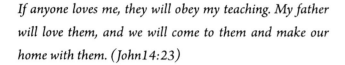

If anyone loves me, they will obey my teaching. My father will love them, and we will come to them and make our home with them. (John14:23)

God, making His *home* with us is the point. When we are loving our neighbor as Jesus instructs, we are also inviting Father to come and make his home with us, keeping our roots firmly planted in his nourishing soil, the way it was intended. He is the source and maintainer of life (Deut30:20). Knowing and living in this love without criticism and judgment towards ourselves and others, is highly contagious. It is also effective for breaking down walls of hurt and anger, while reinforcing a sense of confidence, acceptance, and a Father's *favor,* as we walk it out, and as we work it out, together with him. Love is perfect; it is the highest of all standards. It is an incredible mental, emotional, and spiritual exercise, challenging us to take the high road that we know deep in our souls is the best road, regardless of the strength of the opposition we may be facing. As our Father helps us to win some small battles, we gain the confidence required to engage greater battles. Nothing forms deeper bonds of relationship and confidence in relationships, than when we are fighting together, against a common adversary.

I mentioned a few sentences back how living in God's love without criticism and judgment towards others is effective for breaking down personal barriers and nurtures peace and confidence, as we realize the Father's favor. How does knowing the favor of Father God work, and why do some people feel loved by God and others not so much? I think it is actually rather simple and looks similar to this:

A father has two children, both of whom he loves and displays equal affection and attention. While one of the children responds by wanting to be everywhere and do everything with the father and even begins to imitate the father in a childlike manner, the other child takes for granted the three meals and a roof over their head, is satisfied with the old man's basic provision, isn't too interested in a deeper relationship, and instead spends the bulk of their time sitting in the basement playing video games, surfing the net, hanging out with friends, and eating the groceries father brought home.

———◦———

"Then you will call upon me and come and talk to me, and I will listen to you… (Jer29:12)

———◦———

The child that enjoys the father personally, discovers personal things about the father through natural interaction by time spent together that the other child will only hear of but will never know, leaving his or her view of the father limited, and speculative at best. They will both know the father's rules and they both may even be considered obedient, but only one will ever get to actually know their father and his reasoning, by observing and listening and talking...about anything, everything.

Which of these two children will know the enjoyment of going fishing with their father? Which one will be taught to tune up the garden tractor by the father? Which one will learn how to hunt wild game by the father? Which one will go to lunch regularly with the father? Which one will wind up going on cool adventures? Which one will learn firsthand of what the father loves? Which one will know what to get the father as a meaningful gift on Father's day? Which one will naturally experience and receive continual gifts and gestures by the father simply because they're around him? Which one will have the confidence and really know the peace and the protection and the love of the father personally?

If anyone does not remain in me, they are like a branch that is thrown away and withers. (John15:6)

When the children are younger they won't even notice the difference between each other's interactions and the subsequent relationship with the father until one day one child realizes they are on the outside looking in, as they watch their sibling and their father walking out the door headed out again on another adventure together. While the father has always loved his children equally and wanted a deep relationship with both, sadly, the one child will believe that they are and have always been unloved, with no memory that it was they who for years previously had inadvertently spurned the father, and the relationship is what it is as a result.

———⚬———

As the Father has loved me, so have I loved you. Now remain in my love. (John15:9)

———⚬———

The other child will respond regularly to the father's invitation and as a result, will *experience* more of his goodness, as they increasingly situate their life around his kingdom, remaining in the center of his plans and his presence.

Parting Shot...

The bottom line is that iron does sharpen iron through contact. If you're looking for personal transformation; of becoming the best *you* that you were designed to be, you will find exactly that as you look for God with all your heart. What I think is clear in the scriptures, though, is that God is a God of invitations. He loves, he leads, and he lets. He loves always, and he invites us to himself, in order to lead and direct us into our greatest potential and life purpose. When we refuse his invitation and head off in our own direction, he does not connive, or persist, or manipulate, in order to convince us to remain with him. He is jealous for our relationship but he does not press the issue, and because of his love, he will let us go as we wish.

———◦———

Here I am! I stand at the door and knock. If anyone hears my voice and opens the door, I will come in and eat with him, and him with me. (Rev3:20)

———◦———

I know that may not sit well with everyone, especially those of us who have pursued relationships, have experienced painful rejection, and are now a bit gun-shy in the pursuit of any relationship. Some of us, through broken relationships by the living, or through the death of a loved one, have come to the conclusion that it is better to have never loved than to experience the loss of that love. To you, God said, "I will never leave you or forsake you". I hope you will learn through consistent personal contact with him that he is a faithful Father, and even on your worst day he still believes in you and loves you, and will never leave you alone if that's what you want.

LOVING A FATHER

Nothing is more valued and appreciated in a healthy relationship, than honesty. We hope that *warmth* and generosity would accompany, but if there is no honesty from the outset, there is really nothing there to work from. This is where a culture of conformity, including corporate teaching, corporate singing (we call worship), and corporate prayer, can inadvertently mask and inhibit personal expression and individual thoughtfulness. In other words, in this culture if we don't have our eyes open and looking ourselves for the way, truth, and life, we are susceptible to just going with the flow and doing what everyone else is doing, expecting that since everyone else is doing it, it must be the right thing to do. But what if it isn't? What if it was our natural personal expression, a tiny heartfelt gift, which was most valuable? What if heartfelt was the only thing that mattered?

Loving God is one of the areas of our life that I think has been overlooked, or at very least has been somewhat sullied by personal thoughtlessness, by compartmentalizing in this corporate way. Think about it for a bit. We are dealing with a genuine personality here. Jesus said to speak with God regularly and personally, knowing him as Father. He taught that *true worshippers* would worship God in spirit (dependant on no one else, or any place) and in truth, genuine, recognizing who he is. The apostle Paul taught that we would speak to God continually, and could approach him as a father to a child.

Yes, he is still God, and yes he is creator, and is all-powerful, and is all-knowing, but does that change the fact that he would still want to be loved thoughtfully and honestly by his children who are designed and created in his image? Jesus speaks as though this is very personal, and Father God is inviting us into something very personal with him.

Jesus Christ is the same yesterday and today and forever. (Heb13:8)

Through all the years has God changed? Has his heart changed? At the core, does he want something from his children now that he didn't want before? Did he want something then that he doesn't want now? I don't think so. When I compare what Jesus says to what God spoke through the OT prophets, I think what God was about then, is what he's still about today. Nothing of the old or new should be thrown out.

———⟡———

"Therefore every teacher of the law who has been instructed about the kingdom of heaven is like the owner of a house who brings out of his storeroom, new treasures as well as old." Matt13:52

———⟡———

One day while over at a friend's place this topic of "loving God" came up. I don't know if on that day we came up with any new ground-breaking doctrinal statements, but what I did discover was that a lot of what we "Christians" have practically endorsed as loving, or worship of God, really wouldn't impress all that much if I were Him. In fact, some of it, and maybe even a lot of it, I would personally find quite dramatic and even a bit strange.

When I stopped to think about how I would want my children to show their love for me, their appointed stand-in father, I realized that everything I want from them has to do with quality one on one time spent together, relational harmony with each other, and really nothing more.

In a real and practical sense, they show their love for me by the way they love each other. This is especially true when they lack "feelings" of affection towards each other and when they aren't really *feelin' the love* for each other. I truly want nothing more for all of us than just being a family living in a *competitive-free* zone, enjoying being around each other, and doing pretty much anything together, peacefully. Does a father really want anything more than just peace and quiet, and a relaxed, drama-free harmony? This is why we will go fishing... alone.

The more things change...

When we look through the words that Father God spoke through the prophets as well as the words given through Jesus, it appears as though he may very well see things in a much similar way. Here are two quotes; one found from the old covenant and one from Jesus:

With what shall I come before the Lord and bow down before the exalted God? Shall I come before him with burnt offerings, with calves a year old? Will the Lord be pleased with thousands of rams, with ten thousand rivers of oil? Shall I offer my firstborn for my transgression, the fruit of my body for the sin of my soul?

He has shown you, O man, what is good. And what does the Lord require of you? To act justly, and to love mercy, and to walk humbly with your God. (Micah6:6-8)

And...

So in everything, do to others as you would have them do to you, for this sums up the law and the prophets. (Matt7:12)

More than a feeling...

The words may be different, and the times were certainly different, but the message is identical. Jesus said, that loving our neighbor summarizes the entire law given by God to man, including the words given by God, through the prophets of old. Curiously or not, this new command also encompasses the old *number one*, which is to love God with all our heart, soul, mind, and strength. When we look closely we can see that what Jesus is also doing, is revealing the message or the purpose behind the "old set of family rules."

Jesus is clearly saying then that when we love, regardless of feelings, another human-being, this is a person's primary act of loving or pleasing God. Remember, in this context, affection is something we feel, and love is something we *do* in God.

———◦———

Now remain in my love. If you obey my commands, you will remain in my love... my command is this: love each other. (John15:9-12)

———◦———

Neither Jesus, nor the prophets speak of any other tangible way to love God directly, other than by coming to him, speaking with him, and trusting him by following his instruction. If you were to examine every word that comes from Jesus in the gospels, you will see that his only command including a "new command," deals strictly with the treatment, acceptance, and love for neighbor. When Jesus says, "do not resist an evil person (Matt5:38)", this includes loving a very wide array of people who wouldn't necessarily be thought of as being very *fun-loving*, if we were to follow the teaching and example of Jesus.

In every instance that Jesus speaks in regards to the most important command, he always indicates that loving God and loving neighbor encompasses the entire Mosaic Law and the instruction of God through the prophets. He then typically followed it up by using a parable for the practical application to show how it looks in real life.

Do this...

In the book of Luke, in chapter ten, Jesus is confronted by an "expert of the law", and asked to share his opinion on the question of what a person needed to do in order to gain eternal life. The "expert of the law" asks Jesus, "What must a guy do to inherit eternal life?" Jesus challenges him, and asks, "What is written in the law, and how do you read or understand it?" The "expert" then states that one would "love the Lord God with all your heart, soul, strength, and mind, and love neighbor as self." Jesus replied, "Good answer. Do *this* and live."

Do *this*... Do what?? What is "this"? The guy doesn't ask about worship style or church attendance or fasting, or any other traditional religious act of the day which would seem to be more specific to "God loving". He doesn't skip a beat, but goes straight to part two and asks Jesus; "Who is my neighbor?" Jesus also doesn't put the brakes on and say, "Hold on there cowboy, you missed the first part about loving God, start there." He also talks about the "neighbor".

The *law professional's* question wasn't about whether loving God by loving neighbor was connected in any way or what the difference might be. The prophets spoke clearly to what pleased God, especially Isaiah, Jeremiah, Hosea, and Micah. His question was "Who then do I have to love?" and "How do I have to love them?" in order to keep the command of loving God and inherit eternal life.

It says in the passage that the law expert specifically asked who his neighbor was because he was hoping to justify himself if Jesus would give him the answer he was looking for.

If he was anything at all like the typical "law expert", I imagine this guy just hung out with and "befriended" shiny, cool kids around the synagogue, patting each other on the back, while enjoying cocktails with people who had it together, people like himself. Jesus didn't give him the answer he was looking for. A politically correct Jesus would have told a parable about the *good Jewish law expert,* but true to form, he pulls no punches and cuts straight to the heart of self-justifying religion. He tells the good Jewish law expert a parable, not about the *good Jewish law expert,* but about *a Good Samaritan.* A story about goodness that would magnify a people group considered by the proud Jews as "dogs", being the good neighbor in the story, while the shiny religious folks walk on by and do nothing to help. To make matters worse for the "law expert", Jesus tells him "to go and do likewise", just like the Samaritan "dog".

How did Jesus love his Father and the people he came into contact with day to day? Jesus denied himself a self-centered lifestyle, and lived generously towards his neighbor. He lived his life for the Father's purpose of reconciling all relationships. This was how Jesus loved his Father.

The Son can do nothing by himself; he can only do what he sees his Father doing, because whatever the Father does, the Son does also. For the Father loves the Son and shows him all he does. (John5:19-20)

What was Jesus doing?...

Jesus did anything and gave everything in an attempt to debunk inaccurate perceptions of his Father, while reinforcing his love, approval, and compassion, which had somehow been lost in the words and customs of religion. He did what he did in order to broker peace and fill his Father's Kingdom with the Father's kids.

While some of you may notice that I've failed to also mention sacraments and traditional customs as somehow undercutting the message of loving God, I believe the very opposite is true. Even traditional sacraments are meant to direct us to personal interaction. The "taking-part" and the symbolism alone is meaningless in and of itself. We have often missed the message woven throughout the bible of how it is that we love God, practically, while occupying this planet.

Family ties...

It's no different than you or me having 1 to 7.4 billion kids. What would you really want for your kids? How would they love you? Would it happen by singing songs written by someone else, to you or about you? Or by reciting poetry written by another or agreeing with bold statements about you made by someone else? In part, sure; as children, sure. But a healthy and maturing relationship between a father and child, living in close proximity, will go well beyond canned and impersonal sentiment.

Ask yourself this question: Would you be satisfied if your children's love for you consisted almost entirely of staged sentiment, while they left their other sibling or siblings: hurt, broken, naked, hungry, lonely, and dying? I don't think so.

———◦———

... do you love me? Take care of my sheep. (John21:16)

———◦———

When our kids write us a song from their heart, or personally fashion a poem just for us, or write us a letter of thankfulness, speak directly to us, choose to spend quality time with us, and build up and protect their siblings all by their own choice, but for which we have given instruction along the way, they are loving and honoring us.

If Jesus were still around physically and all were well with the world, I'd love him by helping my wife bake a cake, clean up the yard, and grill him up some choice beef. But he's not, so instead I try to honor him by looking out for the ones he sends *our* way, continuing to do the unfinished work he started, until he gets back and finishes making things all well with the world. He is my friend and I think I would die for him because he not only saved me from myself, but he gave a guy like me value when he called me, "his friend". Living by his way, minus the religion, is as good as it gets ...the peace.... when and as you find it....is a great reward in any world or any kingdom. Do I love him? I hope my actions are reflecting that truth more consistently as I continue to grow up in his love.

Parting shot...

While the religious society of Jesus' day determined that loving God was done by having festivals and singing songs and sacrificing innocent animals and giving ten percent, and not lifting a finger on Sundays, among other customs and rituals, Jesus set the record straight by including love for God and love for neighbor in the same sentence and gave many examples of how that looks.

―――――――――◦―――――――――

The only thing that counts is faith expressing itself through love. (Gal5:6)

―――――――――◦―――――――――

Ultimately, the gauge for knowing how much we love God is calibrated by how it is that we love those around us. How we love those around us is determined by how it is we believe we are loved by God.

PACK LIGHT

Many pages ago we began this journey by taking a look at how things once were before, when we were fully alive, prior to our quest for God-like knowledge. We talked about the typical perceptions of how a person was fed spiritually in the life of God's kingdom, while we also learned the truth of the most vital food according to Jesus. We then moved into identifying the compelling role God's Spirit plays in the lives of individuals who are intent on storing up treasure in God's kingdom by way of Jesus's example for daily living. Then we dove into what and how it is that we can live daily, confidently, and fearlessly as immortals.

We discovered what Jesus's definition of love is and what it is not. It is not a benign, lukewarm affection, and has nothing to do with mutuality, favouritism, initial friendliness, courtesy, or basic appreciation for kind actions. None of that is the kind of love that Jesus was talking about. What we discovered was that love according to God is taking the high road if and when everyone around us is taking the low road.

We explored how it is that followers and friends of Jesus are truly leaders within his Father's kingdom when we are known as lovers and not merely talkers, leading the way as *infected* eyewitness example of a family living in the love of Father-God, exemplifying the personal peace and freedom that can be possessed by mere people who know and walk personally in a Father's love and legit friendship with Jesus.

We came to understand that this walk is not just a theory that is spoken and sung about, but a lifestyle of true and committed friendship. This leads us to understanding better that faith is active and moving, and that without faith it is impossible to please God. We also saw clearly how a Father is pleased when his children display love from a heart that is loved rather than *doing things* out of obligation, habit, or religious motivation.

Dead weight...

All of this has brought us to our final point and conclusion, which in the west at least, may very well be the most difficult aspect of putting this all together, and has railroaded many well-intentioned individuals along the journey.

I want to talk about how we must pack for the journey before us, and how we can be best prepared to go. I can't even begin to tell you how many people I've known personally who have begun the journey well and have come all this way, only to be stopped dead in their tracks by the distractions readily available in this land of opportunity.

Good seed fell among the thorn, which grew up and choked the plants... referring to someone who hears the word, but the worries of this life, and the deceitfulness of wealth choke the word, making it unfruitful. (Matt13:7&22)

One thing that is very clear about Jesus is that he packed light and was always ready to go. In the same way that a mountaineer carefully assembles exactly what he or she needs for the journey, and nothing more, in order to maintain high endurance and agility, we too require endurance, agility, and availability; a light pack is a must. According to Jesus' example, it is extremely important to pack light in order to remain ready and available at all times.

Not long ago I heard a story about a coach who walked into a high-school gymnasium just before a regional basketball tournament and noticed how polished and perfect everything looked. He noticed the custodian making his final inspection and went to him and commended him on his preparations, making mention of how much work must have been involved in getting things ready. The old custodian replied, "Oh, it was not a problem, sir—ya see, I stay ready to keep from havin' to gettin' ready."

On one occasion, as Jesus and his disciples were traveling to Jerusalem, a teacher of the law came up to Jesus and said,

"I will follow you wherever you go." Jesus replied to the man, "Foxes have holes and birds have nests, but the son of man (Jesus was called this) has no place to lay his head. I have no home, and I have no bed. Other than the clothes on my back, I own nothing. My Father will provide as we go. Are you still interested in coming my way, *my* way?"

Time to go...

Later in Luke's gospel, he records a parable that Jesus told of a great banquet, of how a man was preparing and inviting many guests. But now the time had come for the real deal. The preparations had been completed and now it was time for the banquet to get started. The man sent his servant to tell the people who had initially RSVP'd that the banquet was happening now, and that it was time to go.

However, they all began to make excuses about why it was a bad time for them to attend the banquet. Excuses like, "We just got married," and "We're right in the process of building a new house," and "We're working long hours, and are busy running around taking the kids to all their events—so we're really tired this evening and need some 'me' time to just veg and catch up on my show, or post something on Facebook."

We Christians, especially in North America, have come to call this lifestyle of rationalization normal and legit, but I'll be straight up here: Jesus clearly did not. He called it what it is—excuses. He said, in effect, "Not legit, not cool, my friend. Unless you come now while I'm standing right in front of you,

you will walk away and miss it totally." This is more common than not when it comes to human nature and putting some time between making a commitment and fulfilling a commitment. It's easy to say "yes" to helping a friend shingle his roof when it's a month or more away, while every doubt and excuse to not show up typically arises the day before it's time to get it done.

Continuing our story of the great banquet…the servant went back and reported all that he had heard and seen to the master. The master was very saddened and disappointed that his so-called friends had spurned his invitation to the great banquet. Realizing that his *busy friends* felt that their priorities were of greater importance than his banquet, he sent invitations to a group of people who would be less inclined to take him for granted. When he found them, they were, in fact, thrilled to be invited to his banquet.

So the master told his servant, "go quickly into the streets and alleyways and invite the poor, the crippled, the blind, and the lame; go out to the back roads and country lanes, and find the 'bums' and 'hillbillies' and bring them in so that my house will be full. I guess we can count out all the others who claimed to be my friends. Somehow it seems they're all too busy. If they show up late, there won't be room anymore, so don't let them in. They won't get even a taste of my banquet— not even a sniff unfortunately."

A matter of priority...

There's a link between this story and the message in Matthew 6, where Jesus said, in essence, "Don't store up for yourselves treasures of this earth, because the human heart is easily swayed, coveting and obsessing over material things, the comfort of wealth, and the possessions of others. Pack light so you won't inadvertently fall in love with them over what is truly valuable: the Father's plan, the Father's kingdom, and the bringing back together of the Father and his kids."

Paul also reinforces the message of packing light, regardless of whether a person is single or married. He says in 1 Corinthians 7:

"I would like you to be free from concern. An unmarried man is concerned about the Lord's affairs—how he can please the Lord. But a married person is concerned about the affairs of this world and how they can please their spouse—and their interests are divided. I am saying this for your own good, not to restrict you, but that you may live in a right way in undivided devotion to the Lord."

His point is clear if one wants to see it: live in the simplest manner possible so that we might not be distracted and detoured, in order to stay true to our first love through undivided devoted friendship with Jesus and the big picture— God's eternal kingdom already underway.

Now, it's important to read and understand what Paul is saying here correctly. I've heard of instances where husbands and wives have used this passage to justify the leaving of their families for a number of different reasons—some noble, some not so noble. That is not what Paul is saying here. To a married person, living as if they had no spouse means that we are to set that spousal relationship in its right place in light of what is most important, which is friendship with Jesus and living in tune with his purpose.

When my wife's first love is her Father and walks by the Spirit's guidance instructing her to love, since I am the closest person to her, I am a very loved and appreciated man, in spite of my inadequacies and failures. When my eyes are fixed on him and I am attempting to keep in step with his Spirit by intentional interaction, and his Spirit is living in me, and I attempt to see and love her as Jesus loved the church and laid down his life, she is a very loved lady, and not just by human standards that require reciprocity.

She will experience God's love through her husband, who is becoming patient, personally sacrificial and protective in nature. My kids, neighbours and strangers will experience God's love. As I said earlier, the gauge for knowing how much we love God is calibrated by how it is that we love those around us.

Those closest to us by now know all about Jesus and his message of love, at least after this many years knowing us, if we've been what we hope to be, they sure should. Jesus' message is to go and possibly never come back in this lifetime.

Leaving home...

We are surrounded by a local community with many never having experienced the love of the Father. We cannot just stay partying with the one's we know and are comfortable with. A message intended to be visibly lived out cannot spread that way. Jesus isn't telling anyone to stop partying. He's instructing his followers to open up their hearts and lives to all, introducing and encouraging a more spontaneous and inclusive *party culture.*

We've personally had to make tough choices to leave family and move out of comfortable and easy friendships to be a part of developing God's family. I can assure you, it's an uphill battle at times when you choose to run with the *pagans* and *strangers* rather than choosing to visit with *family* and *old friends* on special and not so special occasions.

I ran into an old acquaintance here the other day that I hadn't seen in a few years, while working out at a local fitness center. We exchanged pleasantries but I could tell that he seemed a bit off. When I asked how things had been going, I noticed his eyes were a bit glazed, and he said, "Not good... it's not good at all. I don't know what I'm doing anymore. I just spent thousands on marriage counselling this year alone and I think we hate each other more now than we did before. We've been hating each other for the past ten years and I just can't do this anymore. I hate my life, I feel like I'm dying inside".

The choice is simple and by now the family should completely understand the stakes; life is at stake here. People are not just having bad days. Their lives are crumbling and they are losing hope, because they see no hope, have experienced no hope, and have no hope; often because no one would even give them the time of day. Giving time is the greatest gift of love.

We have to spread our wings and get out of our plush comfy nests and learn to fly into the unknown and learn to enjoy new places of comfort that will provide rest for the weary along life's journey. Today, on every avenue of our travels, there are wars to be won, and we may be running out of time.

We don't need to try to make some huge splash with our life and try to rejuvenate a hundred people all in one go. One for one is all that's required, to just show value and love to the people we encounter, to whatever degree we are able.

We will always have an opportunity to demonstrate God's love. Whether to the cashier ringing in our groceries, the guy who cuts our hair and even the guy that cuts us off in traffic. Those who once may have appeared outwardly intimidating, or rough-looking, asking for spare change on the corner are seen with new eyes, oblivious to appearance and no longer fearful of the unknown.

After reading this book, I encourage you to ask yourself: Do I know how much I'm loved by Father God? Do I know what spiritual food is, and how it is available to me? Do I know and recognize God's Spirit interaction, and role at the very heart of my life? Do I understand the power of living free and the default lifestyle of forgiveness—asking for it, receiving it, and giving it? Are we able to discern between theoretical and practical knowledge when it comes to living out naturally the beauty of the Gospel Message? Are we willing to live beyond our understanding, "recklessly" and against the odds? Can we see that Jesus's style is to love with a selfless, sacrificial, and unconditional love, and that we too will find the greatest joy and freedom by living in the same way? Do we want to run the race in a way, that no matter what level of "training" we're currently at, we're truly running to be the best and to win? Will we throw off all the dead-weight in our lives that hinders our progress in favour of packing light so we can move swiftly and with agility to answer the call of Jesus in every area of our life?

Final Shot...

Father God desperately wants into our lives, and for us to know him personally, intimately, and peacefully, but this is our choice to make. Ultimately you need to come to your own conclusion, because it's your response to that conclusion that will ever have any effect in your life and the lives of those around you. But know this: the time for coddling is over. This is not up to your pastor, priest, or your mother, and has nothing to do with any other person in your life. It's up to you. It's always been up to you.

I cannot think of a better way to end this book than with a reminder of a Father's love and a Father's plan to restore life, with the same words that Joshua gave to the people as they were headed into their promised land.

See, I set before you today life and prosperity, death and destruction. For I command you today to love, to love the Lord your God and to walk in his ways . . .
Deuteronomy 30:15–16

Now choose life, so that you and your children may live and that you may love the Lord your God, listen to his voice, and hold fast to Him,... for the Lord is your life.
Deuteronomy 30:19–20

To my wife, and to my girls, and to those that God has given me audience in this lifetime, I hope you'll choose life. Your Father and maker hopes you'll hold fast to him and him alone; choose life in him and through him, and to him. Your Father is for you; he designed you, so be strong and confident in this, because when you are walking with him and he with you, you will know that you have more than enough to run this race and run it strong.

ABOUT THE AUTHOR

 Kevin M. Blosser is a church leader who works specifically in a transitional role, assisting groups and individuals in their journey from organized corporate conformity into the simplicity of satisfying personal relationship and freedom. Though people may call him "pastor", the reality is that he's just "a guy" working out life and faith personally, while facilitating healthy environments for others to make their own personal faith discoveries. He currently lives with his wife Dana and their two teenage daughters in Alberta, Canada.

CPSIA information can be obtained at www.ICGtesting.com
Printed in the USA
LVOW08s0608150916

504721LV00002B/4/P